A
Handbook
of
Vlax Romani

A
Handbook
of
Vlax Romani

Ian Hancock

The University of Texas
Austin

Slavica Publishers, Inc.

Slavica publishes a wide variety of books and journals dealing with the languages, linguistics, peoples, literatures, history, folklore, etc., of Eastern Europe and the former Soviet Union. For a complete catalogue with descriptions of the books and ordering information, write to:

Slavica Publishers, Inc.
PO Box 14388
Columbus, Ohio 43214

ISBN: 0-89357-258-6

This book was published in 1995.

Printed in The United States of America.

" 'Tis said that their strange gibb'rish tongue
Does to themselves alone belong
Indeed, I oft have heard them speak,
But to my mind it might be Greek:
It is not English, I declare;-
And 'tis not Irish, that I'll swear."

"We cannot tell from whence we came,
And wherefore Gipsy is our name:
Whether from Egypt we have sped,
As many learned men have said,
And thence have Europe overspread;
Or in the wars that did infest,
In former days, th' embattled East;
We have been driven from our home,
And fled in distant parts to roam,
Preserving still our native caste,
That seems by fate ordain'd to last.
Thus we, indeed, appear the same,
As well in character as name;
Maintaining still our ancient nature,
In customs, manners, and in feature;
Speak the same tongue as did supply
Our words through many a century."

William Combe
Doctor Syntax's Visit to the Gipsies
Ackerman: London, 1812

4

Table of Contents

6

8

List of Illustrations and Figures

Preface

The present linguistic description has been compiled from my notes on Vlax Romani grammar prepared for students who are majoring mainly in Asian Studies, Media, Anthropology, Folklore or Journalism, enrolled in the Romani Language and Culture seminar which has been offered each semester at The University of Texas at Austin since 1978. The variety described here incorporates features from a number of kinds of Vlax and, because of that, is not quite like any single spoken dialect.

As it is spoken in the United States and Canada, Vlax adopts items from English very freely, as well as borrowing constructions and translating idioms from that language; this kind of linguistic interference is a natural characteristic of Romani and other diaspora languages, but in preparing this manual reference to the English element has been intentionally minimized, especially where an original (*i.e.* pre-North American) form already exists.

Although this description was originally prepared for students who, in the main, have had a minimum of linguistic training, and who have little or no intention of making use of it beyond the requirements of the course, in its present expanded form its wider purpose is to provide the basis for a Vlax dialect which will be maximally functional in international communication. The codification of a constructed, standardized dialect is currently in progress by members of the Linguistic Commission of the International Romani Union, which was established at the Fourth World Romani Congress held in Serock, Poland, in April, 1990.

Ian Hancock
International Romani Union
Manchaca, Texas 78652-0822, USA

Foreword
Victor A. Friedman
The University of Chicago

Romani is the only Indic language that has been spoken by significant populations in Europe at least since the Middle Ages, and of all the transnational languages of Europe it is territorially the most widespread. Like other languages of Europe, Romani has spread to North, Central and South America, and Australia. Unlike most of the languages of western Europe, but in common with some of the languages of eastern Europe (*e.g.* Albanian and Macedonian), the standardization of Romani has seen significant advances in the course of the twentieth century, although this process for Romani is still in progress. Nonetheless, Romani is currently a language of legal documents, education, mass media and literature in many of the countries where it is spoken. As in the case of languages of other oppressed minorities, it has sometimes been believed that Romani is not a language but a jargon, or that Romani people do not constitute and ethnic group but a social group, a random assortment of individuals, or are an externally-imposed construct (see *e.g.* Willems, 1995). Such misconceptions should not even require attention at the end of the twentieth century, but unfortunately the ease with which information can now be disseminated means that misinformation can be disseminated with equal ease.

    While the various Romani dialects show significant differences, the common core of Romani renders it arguably no less uniform than many European languages with significant dialectal variation. The Roma are no more — nor less — a social group than the Jews or the Irish, and their ethnic identity is no more — nor less — a construct than those of the Germans or Italians. Differences of degree are not the same as differences of kind. It is true that Romani speakers, or the descendants of Romani speakers, differ in the degree to which they identify as an ethnic collective, that some self-identified members of the Romani ethnic group do not have Romani as their first language, and that mutual comprehensibility among Romani dialects will vary according to speakers and situations, but none of these circumstances is peculiar to Romani as opposed to any number of the world's languages and identities.

Hancock's is one of the few Romani grammars written by a Rom. It is also one of the very few written in English. Moreover it is unique in that it represents a supradialectal variety based on the so-called Vlax dialects of Romani spoken in the United States but also used in eastern and western Europe and elsewhere in the Romani diaspora (other such supradialectal grammars, *e.g.* Jusuf & Kepeski (1980) or Cortiade (1988) are based on non-Vlax Balkan dialects).

The name *Vlax* is derived from a Slavic form referring to Wallachia, a region in modern Romania; the Vlax dialects of Romani are characterized, among other things, by a significant Romanian lexical element. In one sense, Vlax Romani is a European language in diaspora, just as are many other languages such as Polish and Norwegian as spoken in the United States, or Macedonian and Greek in Australia. Unlike the case with other languages in diaspora, however, the American variety of Vlax Romani has the potential to contribute significantly to international codification, due to the uniquely transnational nature of Romani culture. As such, this grammar can be seen not only as descriptive, but also as potentially prescriptive insofar as its manner of description supplies a basis for the creation of a supradialectal standard. This work is not intended for the dialectologist who seeks the description of a specific speech community, although scholars with such interests will find plenty of useful data in this book. The facts of dialect variation, both Vlax and non-Vlax, are often noted, and lists of exceptions, while not always exhaustive, point the way for further investigation.

This book is intended as a teaching grammar for students who are studying Romani in order to learn something about it, and/or to be able to use the language for academic and other pursuits. At the same time, the author is aware of the fact that this grammar can be used by Romani speakers seeking to learn about their native language as the object of study and standardization. It is thus also a contribution to the creation of an international Romani standard for use by speakers of the language themselves. This work is of the same use to general linguists and students of Romani dialectology as it is to students of other disciplines; it can prepare them to go out and do fieldwork in the investigation of those questions that interest them. By describing a supradialectal variety rather than a specific dialect, Hancock not only maximizes the potential practical applicability of his material, but serves a variety of academic and non-academic interests for both speakers of Romani and those who wish to learn it. Above all, this work is an introduction to the language of a unique and remarkable group that has survived centuries of persecution with its language and identity intact. The language and its speakers are well worthy of more positive attention than they have so far received from the world at large.

Indian Origins and Westward Migration of the Roma

In India, the word *gypsy* (or *gipsy*), always written with a lower-case initial "g," has been used for the past century to refer to certain migrant or "criminal" classes, without reference to their actual ethnic identity. Grierson's monumental work *The Gipsy Languages of India* (1922) deals, in fact, with the speech of groups as unrelated as the Dravidian Telugu-speaking Bhaṃṭās and the Indo-Aryan Jaipurī-speaking Peṇḍārīs.

Its use in India in this way can be traced to Sir Denzil Ibbetson, an Englishman, who first used it in his 1881 *Census Report for the Punjab*. This is a legacy from the English language which, since the sixteenth century, has used the word to refer to a population which is regarded as one defined by its behavior rather than by its racial and cultural origins. The confusion in the minds of the Europeans about the "gypsy" people is evident in the source of that very word, which is a shortening of *Egyptian*. In Elizabethan English it was written *'gypcian*, and finally abbreviated to *gypsy*.

The word is probably here to stay. It isn't one that is liked very much by a population whose own name for itself is, in Romani spelling, **Rroma** (singular **Rrom**); but at least when it is used, an attempt is made to spell it nowadays with a proper noun's initial capital letter: *Gypsy*.

The reason that Roma are called Egyptians -- not only in English but in Greek (*[E]gyphtos*), Albanian (*Jevg, Magjup*), Macedonian (*Gjupci*), French (*Gitans*), Basque (*Ijito*) and Spanish (*[E]gitanos*) -- and even one Hungarian name for Roma is *Fáraó nép*, "Pharaoh's people" -- is because their arrival in Europe came on the crest of the Islamic wave following the occupation of the Byzantine Empire and south-eastern Europe by the Ottoman Turks. Christian Europe was caught in the grip of an anti-Muslim and an anti-Asiatic paranoia, and with some reason. The Moors had occupied the south-west (parts of Portugal, Spain and France, and the islands of the western Mediterranean), and Poland and Wallachia in the east had also been taken over by the non-Islamic Mongols under Ghengis Khan's grandson Batu. Trade routes to the Orient had been effectively blocked (thus initiating the search for

an alternate route, and the beginnings of European colonialism),
and the Holy Land was no longer accessible to Christian pilgrims.
The Europeans could not, as a rule, distinguish one Mediterranean
or Eastern population from another, and applied names such as
"Turk" or "Tatar," "Saracen" or "Egyptian" indiscriminately. Thus it
was that the Roma, arriving in Europe from the East in the middle
of the 13th Century, acquired the misnomer "Egyptians." Another,
historically related misnomer which has likewise stuck, is "Indians"
for the natives of the Americas, because Columbus thought that
he'd reached the Subcontinent. The Roma were also called "Turks"
and "Tatars," names for them which also still survive today (in
America and Scandinavia respectively). The French called them
Bohemians or *Saracens*, the Germans and Dutch *Heathens* (*i.e.*
Muslims), and the Spanish *Hungarians*, all incorrect ethnonyms.
Only now are Europeans learning to call them by their right name.

    In the countries closest to the Muslims, the Europeans soon
learned that the Roma constituted quite a different population
altogether. Neither Christian nor Muslim, not European, Mongol,
Turk or Semite, they presented the European population with a
real identification problem. They were dark-skinned, and spoke a
language no one had ever heard before, and they seemed to have
no country. In fact, they did know that they had come from India,
and what's more told several people that, but even though we have
records of those encounters dating from the Middle Ages (see
especially Piasere, 1988), the concept of "India" meant little to the
mediæval European peasantry, who found it easier to believe that
the ancestors of the Roma were the Egyptians whom the Bible told
them drove the Jews out of Egypt, or else were those same Jews
being chased. Some also suggested that they were from Atlantis, or
the Moon, or were a "made up" population of individuals who
darkened their skins intentionally with walnut juice, and who spoke
a kind of concocted slang amongst themselves. It wasn't until after
1760, when a theology student at a Dutch university heard some
Malabari (*i.e.* Malayalam) fellow students discussing Sanskrit, that
the Indian origin of the Roma became known to European
academics. That student, a man named Valyi, had learnt some of
the Gypsy language, or *Romani*, from Roma living near his home
in Hungary. He was not a linguist, but he knew enough to realise

that the similarities he perceived between Romani and Sanskrit were of some significance; he passed the information along to others, and by the 19th Century extensive work had begun not only on the Romani language itself, but on trying to determine the origin, identity and history of this Indian population living in the heart of Europe (see Hancock, 1993).

Very many hypotheses were suggested, all limited by the paucity of extensive research materials on Indian languages, and all tainted by the prejudices of their authors, writing in an age of Darwinism and European colonial supremacy over non-white populations. Roma were judged by their contemporary condition in Europe, and it was naturally assumed that this merely reflected their original way of life in India. Our ancestors were described as entertainers and jugglers, prostitutes and thieves, executioners and emptiers of cess-pits.

This view began to spread after 1841, when a man named Brockhaus suggested that since the Romani word for "man" was *Rom*, perhaps this was the same as the Indian word *ḍom* (Pott, 1844:*i*:42). *Ḍom* refers to a class of people which the dictionary describes as

> . . . a very low caste, representing some old aboriginal race,
> spread all over India. They perform such offices as carrying dead
> bodies, removing carrion, and so on.

Very quickly, this became the "conventional wisdom" in Gypsy Studies, and even today is repeated without qualification in books about Roma. While **Rrom** almost certainly does derive from *ḍom*, its original meaning, according to Kenrick (1995:37), was simply "man," in the sense of "us" as opposed to "others," and at the time of the exodus from India did not have Brockhaus' later interpretation. In support of the *ḍom* hypothesis, and also repeated in almost every new study, is the explanation for who the ancestors of the Roma were, why they left India, and when. Based upon the epic *Shāh Nāmeh* by the 11th Century Persian poet Firdausi, the first Roma have, for the past century and a half, been widely supposed to be the descendants of ten thousand musicians and entertainers (another account says 12,000) who were given in the 5th Century AD by King Shankal of Canoj, Maharaja of Sindh, to his son in law, Bahram Gur, a Sāsānian ruler of Persia, as a gift to his court. Their descendants, known as Luri, were still in Persia, according to Firdausi's account, five centuries later. Another suggestion based upon Persian historical records was that a different group of Indians were captured by Ojeif ibn Ambassa, following the death of the Caliph Mamūn in AD 833, and driven northwards towards Aïn Zarba and Khānaqīn north of Baghdād, arriving there some time during the 11th Century. One Arab source refers to this population's being captured by Byzantine troops and then taken northwards into the Byzantine Empire. Yet another hypothesis, put forward by the Dutch Orientalist De Goeje in 1875, was that the ancestors of the Roma were 27,000 Jats captured near Aïn Zarba in AD 855 and herded north into the Byzantine Empire. A further hypothesis, based on the writings of the Arab chronicler Tabari, maintains that Jats from India who had originally settled in the Tigris Valley moved north into Syria some time during the 9th Century.

For the past 20 years, scholars in India such as Rishi, Joshi, Shashi and others have begun to examine Romani history themselves. Linguists in Europe and America, Roma among them, have challenged these historical scenarios repeated by western scholars. For a number of reasons, historical as well as linguistic, an exodus out of India in the 5th Century, with a later arrival in Europe in the 13th Century, doesn't make sense, and while groups originating in India may have left as long as fifteen hundred years ago for the Middle east, their descendants today would more likely be the Nawar or Domari people, and not the Roma who reached Europe in the middle of the 13th Century. We are also now more inclined to believe that while the ancestors of the Roma probably did include Doms, they were only one part of the overall exodus -- camp-followers who went along to take care of the needs of a military force which was put together to resist the spread of Islam into India in the 11th Century.

Between the years 1001 and 1026 AD, Sindh and the Panjab were invaded some seventeen times by a mixed army of Afghani and Turkic troops, called Ghaznavids or Ghazis, led by King Mahmud. Mahmud lived in the city of Ghazni, the capital of the kingdom of the same name which consisted of part of Afghanistan and Khorasan, which is today in eastern Iran. In 1001 they defeated Jayapāla in Afghanistan, bringing an end to the Hindu Śāhi dynasty, and occupied Peshawar in the Panjab, taking half a million slaves; in 1017 they occupied the city of Mathura, birthplace of Lord Krishna, and the first mosque in India was erected. In 1024, Mahmud destroyed the Samanāth Śiva temple and killed 50,000 Hindu troops, and built another mosque. Although the Ghaznavids were ultimately successful (Afghanistan and Pakistan are now Islamic, rather than Hindu, nations, and Kashmir is the only Islamic Indian state), Indian resistance, in the form of Rājpūt troops, was fierce.

The Rājpūts were not historically one people, but an amalgam deliberately created to provide this resistance. They were drawn from the non-Aryan populations of northern India, people called *Pratihāra*, probably descendants of the Scythian invasions a thousand years earlier, and related to the Alani. The camp-followers of these newly-formed legions were drawn from the lowest varṇa (the Śūdra caste), and from the out-caste or untouchable groups such as the Ahirs, the Gujjars, the Lohars, the Lobhanas, the Saudagars and the Tandas. Indian historian R. R. Chauhan (1994) has documented the conscription during this period of large numbers of Siddis or Habshis, Africans from the Horn of Africa and further south who were used as troops by both the Indians and the Muslims; it is not unlikely therefore that an eastern Bantu element might also be identifiable in the makeup of the population which was to become the Roma; it is evident in the Rājput community in India today. An even earlier genetic link between Dravidians and East Africans has been discussed by Rajshekar (1987). The presence of words in Romani which are ultimately of Dravidian origin (such as *e.g.* **kalo** "black," **kuj** "elbow," **čumid**-"kiss," **čhor** "beard," &c.) argues against the suggestion that the ancestors of the Roma separated from an Indic-speaking migration before it reached India -- perhaps in Persia -- an interpretation of history which is today being fiercely challenged by Indian scholars.

All of these groups were selected for their skills, and specifically because they were not Aryans, being drawn from the Dravidian, Pratihāra and possibly African populations. According to Watson (1988:88), these Rājpūts were welded out of different non-Aryan material into a martial society of interrelated families, and rewarded with Kśattriya [warrior] status, and certificates of descent from the sun and the moon

to resist the Islamic encroachment. A remnant of the the symbolic association of these warriors with the sun and the moon, as well as with the stars, is found today among some modern Romani groups in Europe who use them as clan emblems (discussed in Chatard & Bernard, 1959:93-94, and Sutherland, 1975:125). According to Minturn & Hitchcock (1966:11),

> Many of the clans which achieved Kśattriya status are descended from invading tribes that entered India from central Asia prior to the arrival of the Muslims. Later, during the period of Muslim invasions, many of these clans, now calling themselves Rājpūts, or "sons of princes," fled to Rajputana to the south-west of Khalapur...some Rājpūt clans, after offering fierce resistance to various Muslim armies, drifted north or south into the mountainous regions of central India or the Himalayas, and some may have gone as far as Nepal, moving into North India from Central India.

The Rājpūts, of mixed descent but now honorary Aryans, together with their camp followers, probably of mainly Dravidian descent and originating in the Untouchable and Śūdra populations, moved towards the west into Persia, according to Banjara history, through the Khyber, Bolan and Mulla Passes, though recent linguistic evidence suggests a more northerly route out of India, perhaps through the Shandūr and Baroghil Passes. Moving west-wards they became, we can surmise, embroiled in a succession of Middle Eastern confrontations with Islam, moving in a north-westerly direction along the easternmost limit of its expansion. It has been suggested that the impetus for this migration was their defeat at the Battle of Tehrain in 1192 AD, but this would have allowed only a century or less for the population to make its way to Europe, which, while conceivable, is argued against by the extent of Iranic and, particularly, Byzantine Greek, linguistic influence which we would expect would have required a much longer and more in-timate period of contact. As they became more and more remote

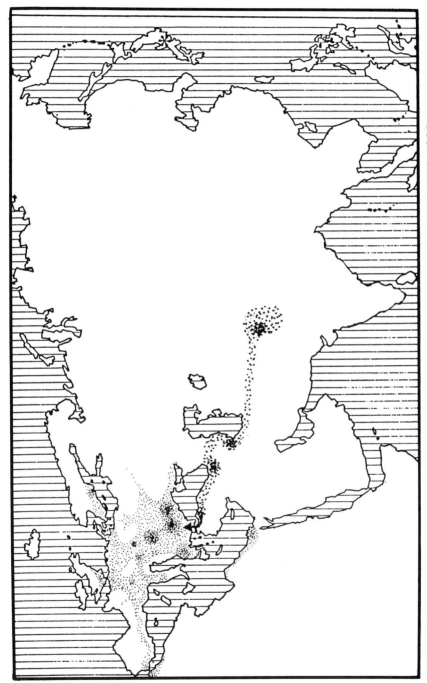

Figure 1: MIGRATORY ROUTE OF THE ROMA OUT OF INDIA, CA. AD 1000-1030

from their homeland, we may surmise that their shared Indian identity overcame whatever newly-acquired jāti or caste distinctions divided them socially; and in time, the population became one. This also provides an acceptable account for the character of the Romani language, which demonstrates Central Indian, Northwestern Indian, and Dardic linguistic characteristics. A 1987 medical report, in the prestigeous British medical journal *The Lancet*, determined that

> analysis of blood groups, haptoglobin phenotypes, and HLA types establishes the [European and American] Gypsies as a distinct racial group with origins in the Panjab region of India. Also supporting this is the worldwide Gypsy language Romani, which is quite similar to Hindi (Thomas, *et al.*, 1987:378).

This had already been acknowledged in a 1977 United Nations Resolution (No. 31.08.1977), which

> recogniz[ed that] Gypsies, or Romanis (*sic*) have historical, cultural and linguistic ties of Indian origin.

The Banjara, who call themselves *Gorwat* or *Gormati*, claim descent from the Rājpūts, and believe that they represent the descendants of the Roma who never left India. They maintain contact with Romani groups in Europe and America, and support a periodical called *Banjara Roma*. Grierson wrote that the Banjara "are originally Dravidian, becoming Aryanized at a comparatively early date, and philological considerations point to the conclusion that this occurred somewhere in Rajputana." Consideration of the Dravidian element in Romani ancestry is nothing new; as early as 1883, the German scholar Richard Pischel discussed this in the journal *Deutsche Rundschau*; but the dual racial heritage of the first Roma, *i.e.* Dravidian and Pratihāra, was not discussed until 1968, when the Romani linguist Vanya de Gila Kochanowski proposed it in his seminal article "Black Gypsies, White Gypsies."

The prominent 19th Century Romanologist Alexander Paspati said that the key to Gypsy history is to be sought in the study of the Romani language, and this is quite true. Romani is, metaphorically, like an onion, because it is built up layer upon layer. Its heart is first of all Central and Northwestern Indian, then there is a layer of Dardic (Hancock, 1988); it is because of the latter, and because there are elements from Burushaski, spoken in the Hunza, that we must locate the area through which the Roma left India in the extreme north of the Hindu Kush (Berger, 1969). In "Burushaski and its alien neighbors," Lorimer (1937:66) wrote

> in the midst of the Burushaski-speaking population, exist small, alien colonies speaking an Indo-Aryan language. . .who are the professional blacksmiths and musicians to the joint communities. They call themselves Ḍoma and their language Ḍumāki, and they are doubtless of the same stock as the Ḍoms of Gilgit.

The next layers are of Persian and Kurdish words, over one hundred of them (see Hancock, 1995), but there are hardly any from Arabic, except through the medium of other languages, thus we can posit a migration westwards along the southern shore of the Caspian Sea which then followed its western littoral up into the eastern Caucasus. Because there are Georgian, Ossetian and especially Armenian words, of which over forty have been identified in the language (le Redžosko, 1984), its speakers must have passed across the southern Caucasus, probably continuing along the southern shoreline of the Black Sea into Europe (the adoption of Turkish-derived lexicon by some south-eastern Romani dialects does not date from this early period).

Because of the massive influence from Mediæval Greek, which has contributed over 200 words, a considerable amount of time was presumably spent in the Byzantine Empire. There was also contact with speakers of Mongolian because of the occurrence in Romani of the single word **mangin** "treasure," (< *mụngụn*), acquired during the trek across the Caucasus or northern Persia during the period of its occupancy by the Golden Horde. Since Mongolian and Turkic languages were not spoken throughout this area until after the mid thirteenth century (Doerfer, 1970:217ff.), and the Romani *aresajipe* or arrival in Europe also took place during this period, we might conclude that the prolonged sojourn of the Roma in the Byzantine Empire was at its eastern, rather than western, end, and that the movement thence into Europe took place fairly quickly.

When we examine these layers, we can also get some idea of the social situation of the Roma; the words for "horse" and "cart," and for "road," (**grast, vurdon** and **drom**) were picked up in the eastern Byzantine Empire, as were the words for nearly all the metals, and for "anvil," "forge," "furnace," "melt," "nail," "horseshoe," "hammer," &c., nearly all of them coming from Greek and Armenian. Nevertheless, three quarters of the basic vocabulary is Indian: eat, drink, run, jump, sit, sleep, up, down, in, out, big, small, hungry, thirsty, aunty, uncle, sheep, snake, cabbage, silver, gold, girl, water, milk, knife, here, there, one, two three, four, five, black, white, red, far, near, joy, guilt, Gypsy man, non-Gypsy man, Gypsy boy, non-Gypsy boy -- all are Indian words (**xa-, pi-, prast-, usti-, bes-, sov-, opre, tele, andre, avri, baro, cikno, bokhalo, trusalo, bibi, kak, bakro, sap, sax, rup, sumnakaj, rakli, pani, thud, čhuri, athe, othe, jekh, duj, trin, star, pandz, kalo, parno, lolo, dur, pas, los, dos, Rrom, gadzo, čhavo, raklo**).

Besides the language, specifically Indian retentions among European, Australian, American, Canadian, Brazilian and other Roma throughout the world are found in all areas of the culture as well. Some groups in Hungary, Slovakia and Transylvania maintain the Indian *bhairāva* musical scale, as well as a type of mouth music known as *bole*, which consists of nonsense syllables imitating the rhythm of the tabla drum; the tribunal where internal disputes are settled, called the **kris** in Romani, while a Greek word, is identifiable with the Indian *panchayat*, and has the same form and function. The **pilivàni** wrestling matches with oiled bodies (*cf.* the Urdu *pehlivān*), and the stick dancing (called **rovljako khelipe** in Romani) are both still found amongst Roma in Hungary; snake-charming (called **fàrmeko sapano**) is a profession among Roma in Serbia; the burning of one's possessions after death and even, among some populations at least into the 20th Century, the ritual suicide of the widow, which has striking parallels with *sāti*. The worship of the goddess Sāti-Sara, who is Saint Sarah, the Romani Goddess of Fate, which forms part of the yearly pilgrimage to La Camargue at Stes. Maries de la Mer in the south of France is of particular significance; Sāti-Sara is the consort of the god Śiva, and is known by many names, *Kāli, Bhadrakāli, Umā, Durgā* and *Syamā* among them. Śiva's trident, called *triśula* in Sanskrit, changed its role from Hindu symbol to Christian symbol and has become the Romani word for "cross" (**trušul**). This probably happened in the 11th or 12th Century, when the migrating Roma reached Armenia; in the Gypsy language spoken there, *t(ĕ)rusul* means both "church" and "priest." Furthermore, the Romani word for "Easter," **Patradji**, is an Armenian word, so this is probably where the Roma first encountered Christianity. Although Hinduism as a cohesive faith has not survived, Roma today practicing a great number of religions adopted because of a historical need to survive, nevertheless many Hindu-based cultural beliefs continue to be strongly maintained. These similarities have been discussed in a number of works by Indian authors themselves, among them Rishi, Bhattacharya, Lal, Shashi and Singhal.

Although eating habits and the techniques of food preparation among the various populations throughout northern India have much in common, it is from Rajasthan and the Panjab that the Roma originated, and it is among the modern-day Banjara that the strongest parallels should be sought. Notions of ritual pollution, central to Romani belief, existed in the varṇa system and continue to exist today; thus members of the same jāti may eat together without risk of contamination, for example, but will be polluted if they eat with members of other jāti; and because the jāti affiliation of one's associates might not always be known, contact between the mouth and the various utensils shared with others at a meal is avoided. In conservative Romani culture (called **Rromanipe**), liquids are poured into the mouth from a container held away from the lips, so that the rim of the vessel (the **kerlo**) is not touched; smoke from a shared tobacco pipe is drawn (in the Romani language **pilo** or "drunk," rather than "sucked") through the fist clenched around its stem, again to avoid contact by the mouth. The surest way to avoid contact with utensils used by others, is to eat with the fingers, and all of these habits are to be found among Roma today. Like the Rājpūts, the Roma divide foods into "ordinary" and "beneficial" or "lucky" (**baxtalo**) categories (the Rājpūts call them "cold" and "hot" foods, though this has nothing to do with temperature or pepper). Similarly, and again like the Rājpūts, Roma divide illnesses into those which are natural to the group, such as heart conditions or irritability, and those which are the result of over-familiarity with the **gadže** or outsiders. These latter include, for example, all sexually-transmitted diseases. For such afflictions, a non-Gypsy physician must be consulted; but for "Romani afflictions," traditional cures are provided by a **drabarni** or female healer. This is the same as the Rājpūt *sīana*. The root of the word *drabarni* is **drab** which means "medicine" (from Sanskrit *dravya* "medication," compare Hindi *darb*). It is also the root of the verb √**drabar-** which is usually translated in English as "to tell fortunes," but which from the Romani perspective means "making well." When speaking English, Roma prefer to call this skill brought from India "advising" rather than "fortune telling," for which another verb, √**duriker-**, exists.

It is in the area of spiritual and physical well-being that the Indian origin of the Romani people is most clearly seen. In the preparation of food, and in one's personal hygiene and deportment, it is absolutely essential that a separation between "pure" (**vužo**) and "polluted" (**makhardo** or **pokhelime**) states be maintained. A pure state is achieved by maintaining "balance" (**kintàla**) in one's life; maintaining balance or harmony pleases the spirits of the ancestors (the **mule**), and they are there to guard one and help one do it, but if they are displeased, they will mete out punishment by way of retribution (**prikàza**). The penalty for extreme pollution is banishment, or becoming outcast, and an out-caste, from the community, for which the Romani words are **marime** and **gonime**. *Prikàza* brings bad luck (**bibaxt**) and illness (**nasvalipe**), and it can be attracted even by socializing with people who are not **vuže**. This includes all non-Romani people or **gadže** (singular **gadžo**, from Prākrit *gajjha* which means "domestic," "non-military" or "civilian"), and that is why the Roma have so successfully kept their separateness -- and as a result their identity -- for so long, and why they will continue to do so.

The Dialects of Romani

During the seven or eight hundred years that it has existed in Europe, the Romani language has become fragmented into many

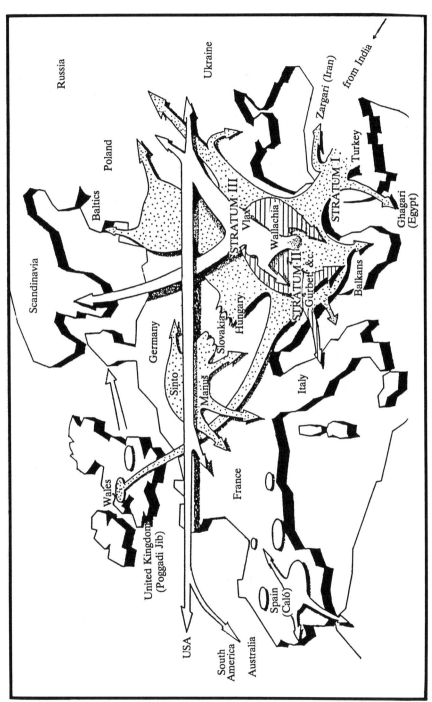

Figure 2: DIFFUSION OF THE ROMANI DIALECTS (AFTER CORTIADE, 1991:12)

different dialects. There are sixty or more of these, although they all fall into just five or so groups. The cluster of dialects known as Vlax (or Vlach, Wallachian or Danubian) emerged during the five or six hundred years during which Gypsies were kept as slaves in Wallachia and Moldavia, former principalities which today constitute parts of modern Romania. The other, non-Vlax branches have developed among populations which did not remain in those lands, or perhaps, like the Gümülcine in Turkey, never even reached them. But those who moved on through the Balkans had spread out into northern and western Europe as early as the 14th Century, reaching every western country by about AD 1500. This spreading-out of those not held in slavery is referred to as the First European Romani Diaspora. Some intermediate dialects are spoken by populations who remained longer under the linguistic influence of Romanian; the Welsh Romani dialect, for example, present in the British Isles since at least the mid-1700s, contains some twenty lexical items of Romanian origin, has the negated *BE*-form **naj**, and includes lexicalizing elements such as the prefix {**vare-**} (*cf.* both Welsh and Vlax Romani **varekaj** "somewhere," **varekon** "someone"). Inflected English Romani, spoken in the British Isles into the 20th Century, also included vocabulary items of Romanian origin, and a small class of plurals formed with the Romanian-derived {**-uri**} (see pages 147-148, and Hancock, 1984:103). A discussion of the diffusion and characteristics of the different branches of Romani is found in Hancock (1988) and Cortiade (1994); a complete classification of all the existing Romani dialects has still to be achieved, though work on this is in progress. The diagram on pages 32-33 is adapted from Kaufman (1979).

Since the end of slavery in the middle of the 19th Century, speakers of the Vlax dialects have taken them to all parts of the world; to every country in Europe, as well as to North, Central and South America, and to Australia. Vlax speaking communities are to be found in eastern China, South and East Africa, and Singapore and Hong Kong as well. This 19th Century diffusion of the population is referred to as the Second European Romani Diaspora. Of all the different kinds of Romani, the Vlax dialects have the most speakers and are spoken in the greatest number of countries around the world. It is an appropriate choice, therefore, as the type of Romani which will be most widely useful to the learner. It is also the variety for which most dictionaries, grammars and non-linguistic texts have been published.

The Vlax dialects are very similar to each other, and having learned one, learning any of the others may be accomplished with little adjustment. Its main dialects are Russian Kalderash, Romanian Kalderash, Serbian Kalderash, Machvano, Lovari and Churari, although these are not all of them.

In the United States, Australia, Argentina and Brazil, the two most widely-spoken varieties of Vlax are Machvano and (especially Russian) Kalderash, this latter also known as Coppersmith or Călderari Romani. While the label *Machvano* refers to a specific geographical area (around the town of Mačva, in eastern Serbia, from which the ancestors of the Machvaya came), the name *Kalderash* was originally an occupational label, meaning "maker of (copper) kettles," and therefore does not refer to a original, locally-developed dialect. The speech of those Coppersmiths who left Romania in an easterly direction is characterized by extensive Russian (and Belorussian and Ukrainian) influence, while the dialect of those who migrated out towards the west is marked by lexical adoption from Serbian especially. The phonologies of the eastern and the southern Slavic languages, as well as of the eastern and the western dialects of Romanian, have also influenced the development of the different varieties of Vlax, so that Serbian Kalderash is far more like Machvano than is Russian Kalderash. Apart from those which developed internally (see *e.g.* Hancock, 1990), features distinguishing the dialects are those acquired from the different languages with which Vlax speakers have been in contact since the Second European Diaspora following emancipation in the 1850s and 1860s. In a wider sense, this process has been going on in Romani since the time of the First European Diaspora; it is this non-core, or accreted, linguistic material which constitutes the greatest barrier to inter-intelligibility, and one of the tasks of the Language Commission established at the Fourth World Romani Congress held at Serock, near Warsaw, in 1990 was to create an international standard and to cultivate a greater use of such core forms. Examples of these are given on pages 171-172.

32

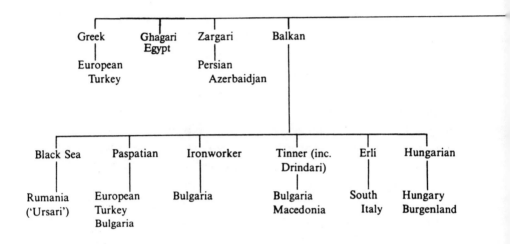

Figure 3: THE BRANCHES OF ROMANI (AFTER KAUFMAN, 1979:131-144)

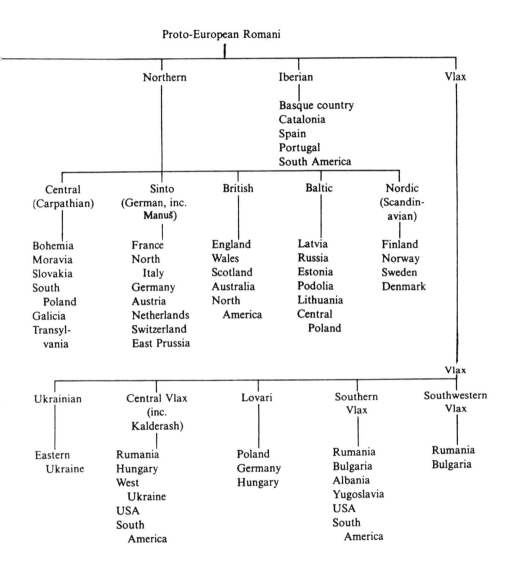

Romani Spelling

It is a commonly-repeated fallacy that Romani is not a written language. It has, in fact, been written for over a century, admittedly mainly by non-Gypsy scholars studying and describing it, and who have used a variety of scientific, phonemic orthographies. Some of the earliest extended texts in Romani of this type have been scriptural translations or collections of folk-tales. But since at least the last quarter of the 19th Century, a steadily-increasing number of individuals, native speakers themselves, have attempted to set the language down on paper for their own purposes. These have mostly taken the form of personal letters, common among the non-Vlax Bashalde Roma in the north-eastern part of the United States in the decades following their immigration into this country following the collapse of the Austro-Hungarian Empire; members of the Russian Kalderash (Vlax) family of Nickels also have in their possession letters written from Russia during the 1920s to relatives in America, in Romani written in Cyrillic characters; the Texas Romani Archives contains copies of works by Pushkin and Merimée also in Romani in Cyrillic orthography, and published in the 1930s. Since the end of the Second World War, use of the written language has been extended to include newspapers, biographies, collections of poetry, historical treatises, political addresses and so on, and since the opening up of eastern Europe following the collapse of Communism in 1989, the production of Romani-language books and magazines has flourished. Romani is the official language of the World Romani Congress, and is used in its various dialects by such organizations as The Rom & Cinti Union, The International Roma Federation and the Press Rom News Agency in their internal correspondence. A multi-volume Romani-language encyclopædia is also in the process of compilation.

These formalized examples of the written language aside, the practice, when it is written by people who speak it, as opposed to outsiders who study it, has usually been to employ the only spelling known to them, namely that of the principal language of the country in which those speakers live. Thus at the present time, the overwhelming majority of Romani speakers in an English-speaking country, if literate, will have become literate only in English; in a

French-speaking country, only in French, and so on. And if they attempt to write in Romani, they will adapt a spelling from the only system they know -- that is, from English or French. Thus the word for "can" or "able" might be spelled *shy* or *shie* by an American Rom, writing the word as if it were English, while a Rom in France using French spelling conventions might write the same word as *chaille*. In Germany it would be written *schei*, in Poland *szaj* and so on. While each spelling would work in its own country, if an American Rom writing to a Rom in France or Germany or Poland were to spell the word "shy," it would probably be pronounced as "see" by those speakers and not be understood. A speaker of American Romani reading the French spelling of the same word would probably make it rhyme with "mile," and likewise not understand what was meant.

SCHEJ BEN SOSTE MAN CHOCHAWES   (*čhej phen soste man xoxaves*
SCHEJ BEN SOSTE MAN DILARES   *čhej phen soste man diljares*
SCHANES SOSTE ME GAMAV DU   *džanes soste me kamav tu*
GA NEI AWER SCHUGAR SAR DU   *ke naj aver šukar sar tu*
ME DRADAW ANDA DUTE DUR   *me tràdav anda tute dur*)

Example of German-based orthography: the printed lyrics inserted with a compact disk of Romani songs produced in Austria (Stojka, 1994, reprinted with permission)

Figure 4

    The policy of the International Romani Union is to have one standard spelling so that any Romani speaker anywhere in the world can learn and use it, and anyone else who has also learnt it could then read it and pronounce it correctly. But this can only happen once the creation of a standard dialect, with a more or less agreed-upon pronunciation, has been completed. The Linguistics Commission of the International Romani Union is developing such a dialect, and has already created a standardized phonemic orthography, discussed below, which will eventually be used for the standardized International Romani.

The standard alphabet makes use of a number of new (*i.e.* non-traditional) graphemes, such as <ç>, <θ> or <8>, <q> and <3>. Meanwhile, there are two other systems which are now in use, which will also be described here: *a*) a Pan-Vlax orthography for international correspondence which uses letters with diacritics, and *b*) a modification of it which substitutes English-based combinations of letters and no accent-marks, for use specifically by Vlax speakers in English-speaking countries. It would be a good idea to learn all three methods of spelling: Pan-Vlax (*PV*), English-based (*EB*) and International Standard (*IS*). The Pan-Vlax system is the one used in this book, and which is described in detail below.

Stress

In Vlax, the stress usually falls on the last syllable of the word, and if such words take enclitic morphology, the stress remains predictable according to the rules which govern its distribution. In this book, stress is not indicated where it is root[1] or stem[1] final, or where it is predictable. Thus where a simple item has no written grave accent (`), it can be assumed to have final stress: **rakli, balo** (= **raklì, balò**), &c. Likewise the inflected forms of such words predictably maintain stress on the same syllable: **rakljàsa, balèndar.**

The stress placement of many words, and especially on *athematic* items, however, cannot be predicted, and in these cases it is shown throughout with a grave accent over the syllabic vowel. In most instances, stress placement on the lexical form is simply the result of inheritance from the donor language, but it may also have grammatical function, thus **phràla** "brother!" (vocative[1]), *vs.* **phralà** "brothers" (plural), **gàzda** "boss" (subject case[1]) **gazdà** "boss" (oblique case[1]"), **tràdas** "we travel," **tradàs** "he travelled," **bilàvel** "it melts," intransitive, **bilavèl** "it melts," transitive. Marking the stress on polymorphemic items as is sometimes done in this book (*e.g.* on the pluperfect verbs) is only a learner's guide; it is not indicated in ordinary writing except in cases where it becomes necessary to disambiguate or to indicate non-predictable stress.

---

[1]These terms are explained on pages 54 and 55.

Vowels

\<a\> This usually has the "Continental" value, *e.g.* as in Spanish *la muchacha*. Example **rat** "blood."

\<e\> Somewhere between the English /e/ in "red" and Spanish /e/ in *huevo*; never a diphthong as in *they*, except in some song styles. Example **mel** "dirt."

\<i\> Usually like the /i/ in Spanish *mi, cinco*. Example **trin** "three."

\<o\> As in Spanish *dos* or French *eau*, and never a diphthong as in English, except in some song styles. Example, **mol** "wine."

\<u\> Usually as in Spanish *luna* or French *vous*, never a diphthong as in English, except in some song styles. Example, **tumen** "you (plural oblique).

\<j\> In PV and the SI orthographies, this represents the English sound /y/, and never the English /j/ sound in *judge* or *jump* or the French sound in *jamais* or *rouge*. In the English-based system used in the United States, however, it has its English value. It is both a consonant and a vowel in Romani, thus **jag** "fire," **baj** "sleeve."

\<v\> This is also both a glide and a fricative in Romani. Its articulation for very many speakers is something like an English /w/, except that it is made with the top teeth *behind* the lower lip (phonetic [ʋ]), instead of in front of it. Thus **voliv** "I love" sounds rather like "woliw." Some speakers, of western Vlax especially, pronounce this more like [voliv].

In Vlax, because of many centuries of influence from Romanian, some of these vowels have become centralized or unrounded in some environments, *thematic* ("native") as well as those adopted from Romanian, thus /i/ will become /ɨ/ following /rr/. It is not necessary to show this in writing, since the feature has no bearing upon the meaning of the word. If it is necessary to indicate these reduced vowels for the purpose of the learner, these features may be shown in a number of ways, *e.g.* by placing a dot below (as in this volume), or a dierasis above the letter, thus \<i̧\>, \<ï\>, \<ạ\>, \<ä\>, or by introducing a new letter altogether to replace all of the modified forms. Some publications have used <ə> or <ъ> for this; others have used the superfluous letter <y>. The /i/ in **trin** "three," for example, is not the same as the retracted /i/ in **sim** "I am," the /u/ in **tumen** "you" is not the same as the unrounded /u/ in **ljùmja** "world," and the /a/ in **sam** "we are" is not the same as the centralized /a/ in **mùca** "cat." Some earlier wordlists have represented these different sounds with the same symbol: **sъm, ljъmja, mùcъ**.

Another feature resulting from phonological interference from the coexisting European language is the /j-/ acquired by initial vowels in Russian Kalderash, thus **jamaro** "our" (for **amaro**), **jertisar** "forgive" (for **ertisar**). This has affected Kalderash in Russia, but is not a feature of the same dialect as spoken in the Americas.

Diphthongs

Diphthongs are sequences of two vowels. In Romani, the "falling" diphthongs are /aj/, /oj/, /uj/, /ej/ and /ij/:

<aj> This is like the /ai/ in *Cairo*. Example **naj** "finger."

<oj> Like the /oi/ in *oil*. For example **gunoj** "garbage.

<uj> Like the "ouie" in *Louie*. Examples **kuj** "elbow," **cùjka** "brandy."

<ej> This is like the /ey/ in English *they*. Examples are **dej** mother," **phej** "sister," **mèjva** "fruit."

<ij> Like the "ee" in *tree*. Example, **hertìji** "documents."

There are also "rising" diphthongs, with the vowels in the reverse order of these (<ja>, <jo>, <ju>, &c.), for example **fjàlo** "kind (of), sort (of)," **pherdjol** "it's getting full."

Consonants

<c> This is like the "ts" in *cats* , and never as in English. Examples include **cincàri** "mosquito," **cìrde** "pull!," **njàmcicka** "German language."

<č>   Like the "ch" in *inches*, rather than like the "ch" in *church* or *cheese*, which have more expression of air accompanying their release. Example **čačo** "true." This extra air is called aspiration, and it is an important characteristic of Romani phonology. See next, and also <kh>, <ph> and <th> below.

<čh>   This is like the **č** above, except that it is articulated with the tip of the tongue retroflexed, *i.e.* curled back towards the roof of the mouth, producing a sound something like "shr" or even "tr." For some speakers this has become a "sh" sound (as in *shoe*) entirely. Examples include **čhej** "(Romani) girl," **lačho** "good." This sound corresponds to an aspirated /č/ (/č/ + /h/), its original value.

<d>   This is made with the tip of the tongue touching the back of the top teeth, *i.e.* it is a dental sound as in Spanish, and not alveolar as in English, where the tip of the tongue makes contact higher up, above the back of the top teeth. Example **dand** "tooth."

<dj>   This is a sound not found in English, and is made by bringing the middle of the tongue up against the roof of the mouth to produce a sound somewhere between the "dy" and "gy" in, for example, *did you* and *dig you*, e.g. in **kerdjol** "it is made." For many speakers, it has become the "j" sound in English *judge* or *jump*. The digraph <**gj**> sounds the same as <**dj**>.

<dž> This combination of letters represents the "zh" sound in the English words *Zhivago* or *mirage*, or in the French words *jamais* or *siège*, but articulated with the tongue-tip retroflexed so that it sounds something like "zhr" or even "dr" (*cf.* <čh> above). Speakers of Machvano Vlax pronounce it this way especially; some speakers of eastern Kalderash pronounce it without retroflexion, as "zh" (see <ž>, below). Examples are **gadžo** "non-Rom," **džanènas** "we had known."

<f>   As in English. **fòro** "city." It alternates with other sounds for some speakers, thus **buflo** ~ **buxlo** "wide," **ful** ~ **khul** "excrement."

<g>   This always represents the "g" in *give*, and never as in *giant*.

Example: **gịndiv** "I think."

<gj>   The same as <dj>, above. Example **gjệrco** "a mouthful of liquid; a gulp."

<h>   This is like an English "h." Examples include **mahàla** "neighborhood; crowd," **hamome** "mixed." Speakers of eastern Vlax in Europe often pronounce the <h> as a <x>, including after stops, thus **xatjarav, pxuv** "I understand," "ground," (for **hatjarav, phuv**). See <x>, below.

<j>   In the Pan-Vlax orthography used here, this is the same as English "y," and never like "j" in *jump*. See the discussion for this sound above at page 37.

<k>   This is like the English "k" in *poker*, and never as in *kiss*, which has a puff of air accompanying its release. This would be written <*khis*> if it were a Romani word. Examples are **kànden** "they obey," **kaj** "where."

<kh>   This is an aspirated sound, *i.e.* a "k" followed by a strongly-breathed "h," as in the *k + h* combination in the word *cookhouse*. Examples are **khànden** "they stink," **khaj** "fart."

<kj>   This is a sound not found in English, and is made by bringing the middle of the tongue up against the roof of the mouth, to produce a sound somewhere between "ky" and "ty" as in for example *thank‿you* and *bet‿you*. E.g. **kjìpo** "image, figure."

The digraph <tj> has the same sound. Some speakers pronounce this as <č>.

<l>   A kind of "l" made at the back of the tongue, as in *blue*, rather than at the front of the tongue as in *leaf*. An example is **love** "money." It has this value in all positions.

<lj>   Like other combinations of consonants with /j/, this is just one sound in Romani, not two, *i.e.* it is not a sequence of <l> + <j>. The sound is found in Spanish, where it is represented by <ll>. It is made by pressing the middle part of the tongue up against the palate while making an /l/. It also occurs in French, as in *lieu*, and Italian, in *voglio*. A Romani example is **ljụljàva** "tobacco pipe." If this were divided into syllables, it would be pronounced /**ljụ-ljà-va**/, not */**ljụl-jà-va**/.

<m>   As in English. Examples are **murro** "my," **kham** "sun."

\<n\> The tongue touches the back of the top teeth when making this sound, and not the gum above them as for an English /n/. This is a dental sound, like \<d\> and \<t\>. Example: **naj** "there isn't," **kan** "ear."

\<nj\> This is like the \<ñ\> in Spanish *mañana*, and not like the sequence of /n/ and /y/ in the English word *canyon*. It is also found in French (*agneau*), Italian (*gnocchi*) and Portuguese (*manhã*). A Romani example is **ponjàva** "carpet;" if this were divided into syllables it would be pronounced /**po-njà-va**/, and not */**pon-jà-va**/.

\<p\> Like the English /p/ in *upon*, that is, without the puff of air following it (as, for example, in the word *pay*). This aspiration is an /h/, and would need to be shown in Romani spelling: **phej**. Compare this word, which means "sister," with **pe**, which means "on."

\<ph\> This is the /p/ sound with a strong puff of air following it. Do not confuse the Romani digraph \<ph\> with the English one, which sounds like an /f/ (as in *phone*; this word would have to be written *foun* in Romani orthography). Example: **pherav** "I fall down" (compare with **perav** "I fill up").
\<ph\> is pronounced \<px\> by some speakers in Russia and Poland.

*/q/ There is no "q" in the Pan-Vlax system of spelling, although it is used in the International Standard Orthography (see page 44). The sound it represents is written as \<kv\> or \<ku\>, thus **kvìbo** or **kùjbo** "nest, core, heart."

\<r\> This is something like the Spanish \<r\>, and is made with the tip of the tongue. It is never rolled like the /r/ in American English. Examples are **raj** "gentleman," **čorimos** "theft," **bar** "fence, outside wall."

\<rr\> This is something like a French \<r\> as in *très*, *rouge*, &c., made in the back of the throat. Examples which contrast with \<r\> are **rraj** "twig, branch," **čorrimos** "poverty," **barr** "rock, stone."

\<š\> This is the same as the English /sh/ sound in *sheep*, and is made without curling back the tongue (see \<čh\>, above). Compare the two words **šel** "hundred," and **čhel** "smallpox."

\<t\> This is made with the tongue touching the back of the teeth, and not like an English /t/, where the tip of the tongue is higher up (*cf.* <d> and <n>, above). There is also no /h/ sound following it as there usually is in English; compare **tu** "you," and **thuv** "smoke."

<th> This is the last sound <t> followed by a strong release of air. Don't confuse the Romani digraph with the English one; the word **thulo** "fat" doesn't begin with the same sound as English *think*, which is not found in Romani.

<tj> The same as <kj>, above.

<v> Something like a /w/ for most, though not all, speakers. See the note for this sound on page 37, above. Some speakers pronounce this like an English /v/ in all positions, while speakers of Machvano Vlax hardly pronounce it at all, especially after an <o> or a <u>, as in **vov** "he," **šov** "six," **thuv** "smoke," **phuv** "ground."

*/w/ There is no /w/ in this system of spelling; use <v> instead.

<x> This is quite different from the English <x> which would be written <ks> in Romani: **tàksa** "tax;" it sounds like the <ch> in German *Achtung* or Scots *loch*. Examples of words with this are **xas** "we're eating," **xoxaven** "they're telling lies." For some speakers, this sound has fallen together with <h>.

*/y/ There is no /y/ in this orthography. Use <j> instead.

<z> Like the English <z> in *zoo, hazy*. Examples from Romani are **zumi** "soup," and **zumaves** "you're trying."

<ž> This is the "zh" sound in *Zhivago* or *pleasure* or *mirage*, distinct from the sound written <dž>, *q.v.*, which is retroflexed. Some examples are **žòja** "Thursday," **ažutil** "she's helping."

Variant Orthographies

In most publications in Romani which originate in eastern Europe, <h> is used for both <h> and <x>. In such spelling, <hamo> can represent either **hàmo** "harness," or **xamo'** "food." In Romania, [ʒ] is represented by a <j>, thus <jamba> for **žàmba** "toad;" both <dž> and <dj> are represented by <g> followed by <e> or <i>, for example <geli>, <gianav> for **djèli** "thing," džanav "I know," and <č> is similarly shown by a <c> followed by an <e> or an <i>: <ciacio> for čačo "true." <c> and <š> are indicated by writing a cedilla below /t/ and /s/ respectively: <ţera> for cẹrra "a little," <şai> for šaj "can, able." In Hungary, there is an increasing use of the English digraphs <sh> and <ch> to represent <š> and <č>.

The phonemic distinction between <r> and <rr> is not usually shown orthographically, although the latter can appear variously as <ř>, <ȓ> or <ɽ>. Similarly, few publications yet represent the distinction between the retroflexed and non-retroflexed pairs <čh>/<š> and <dž>/<ž>, although material originating in Sweden has done so using an acute vs. a wedge accent: <śel> and <šel> for čhel and šel "smallpox," "hundred," <źan-ba> and <žamba> for džan-ba and žàmba "go!," "toad." Publications from Serbia use <ć> and <č> to distinguish between <kj>/<tj> and <č>.

The English-based Spelling

Romani language publications produced in the United States and Canada use a modified version of the PV alphabet, which substitutes English letters and letter combinations for those which have accent marks. It does not indicate stress placement, and the digraphs <sh> and <zh> each stand for two distinct phonemes. The equivalents are:

<c> Is <ts>: mutsa "cat."
<č> Is <ch>: chacho "true."
<čh> Is <sh>: lasho "good."
<dj> Is <j>: juso "orange juice."
<dž> Is <zh>: zhanel "she knows."
<j> Is <y>: yertisar ma "excuse me." In diphthongs, it is written <i>: gunoi "rubbish," shai "can, able."
<lj> Is <ly>: zhalya "grief."
<nj> In <ny>: nyanya "auntie."
<š> Is written <sh>: shel "hundred."
<rr> Should also be written <rr>, though it is often represented by a single <r>. The digraphs <rh> and <gh>

have also been used (<**Rhom**> or <**Ghom**> for **Rrom**, "man").

<v>   Is also properly written <v>, but /w/ often takes its place, for example in the given names **Vòšo** or **Vànja**, which are sometimes written as **Wosho, Wanya**.

<ž>   Is <zh>: **azhutimos** "assistance."

Speakers of dialects which pronounce <dj> and <tj> as <g> and <k>, *e.g.* Russian Kalderash, use those letters in their spelling: **stagi, buki** (for **stadji, butji**) "hat," "work."

The International Standard Spelling

The Language Standardization Commission of the International Romani Union has developed a spelling intended to be used for the new standardized dialect, which is also in the process of being codified. It is already employed in the publications being produced by Rromani Baxt in Poland (e.g. *Informaciaqo Lil*), and Interface in France (see e.g. Hill, 1993, 1994, 1995), and is the orthography used in the Romanian-language Romani grammar by Sarău (1994). It is also the orthography in which the multi-volume *Bari Enciklopèdija Rromani* will appear. Its principal features are:

<č>   Is <ć>: **ćùnrri** "braids."
<čh> Is <ćh>: **ćhudo** "thrown."
<dj> Is <dź>: **dźeźeś** "locomotive."
<dž> Is <ʒ>: **ʒangle** "they knew."
<r>   Is <r>: **Ròma** "Rome."
<rr> Is <rr>: **Rroma** "Gypsies."
<š>   Is <ś>: **śuvlo** "swollen."
<ž>   Is <ź>: **źìvina** "animal."

The consonants in the postpositions {-**tar**}, {-**ke**} and {-**k-**} undergo voicing following a preceding /n/ (*i.e.* to {-**dar**}, {-**ge**} and {-**g-**}; see page 66-67), while the postposition {-**sa**} is affricated to {-**ca**}. In the IS orthography, these consonants are non-variably represented by <θ>, <q> and <ç> respectively: **tuθar** "from you" (sg.), **tumenθar** "from you" (pl.); **lesqe** "for him", **lenqe** "for them;" **gaʒesqo** "man's," **gaʒenqo** "men's;" **tuça** "with you" (sg.), **tumença** "with you" (pl.). In PV orthography, these are written **tutar, tumendar, leske, lenge, gadžesko, gadžengo, tusa, tumenca.**

<jo> and <ja> are written <ŏ> and <ă> with a wedge accent, called a *čhiriklo* in Romani, when they consist of two morphemes, or where the presence or absence of the palatalization reflects a dialectal variation, thus **barŏl** "it's growing," **ʒanglăm** "we knew." These are pronounced **barol** and **ʒanglam** in some dialects (notably Lovaritska), but are written and pronounced **barjol** and **džangljam** in the present study.

Although not part of the *IS* orthography, <w> has been incorporated into it by some writers to represent vocalized <v> (thus **abăw** "wedding"), and <ə> to incorporate the various dialect differences in the first person singular present and preterite verb endings: **səm** "I am," for **sim, sem, som,** &c.; **dikhləm** "I saw," for **dikhlem, dikhlom, dikhlum,** &c.

Stressed syllables when not final or predictable are indicated by a grave accent (`) as in the PV orthgraphy.

Centralized and unrounded vowels are indicated with a dierasis: **rrïnza** "chitterlings."

Instead of an apostrophe to indicate contractions, a hyphen is used: **and-o** for PV **and'o** (**ande o** "in the"), **ć-o** for PV **tj'o** (**tjiro** "your", sg.).

Vocative (direct address) case endings are preceded by an exclamation mark, thus **ćhave** "boys," **ćhav!ale** "hey, boys!," **bibi** "aunt," **bibi!o** "hey, aunty!", **Rajìda** "Rita," **Rajìd!o** "hey, Rita!."

Questions are signaled as in Spanish by an inverted question mark at the beginning of the sentence in addition to an upright question mark at its end: ¿**sar bućhos**? "what's your name?".

The second person singular and plural personal pronouns are capitalized: **lośeno sim te dikhav Tut** "I'm happy to see you."

Names of days, months and seasons, and adjectives of nationality, are not capitalized: **patradźi** "Friday," **decèmbro** "december," **nilaj** "summer," **francuzicko** "French." These lists are given in full on pages 106-107.

Text in Three Orthographies

PV	me	či	džanav	kaj	si	m'e	dadeski	kat,	nùma
EB	ME	CHI	ZHANAV	KAI	SI	M'E	DADESKI	KAT,	NUMA
IS	me	ći	ʒanav	kaj	si	m-e	dadesqi	kat,	nùma
	I	*not*	*know*	*where*	*are*	*my*	*father's*	*shears,*	*but*

PV	pučhava	tutar	tjirjake,	ke	vušòro	mjazos
EB	PUSHAVA	TUTAR	CHIRIAKE,	KE	VUSHORO	MIAZOS
IS	pučhava	Tuθar	Tïrăqe,	ke	vušòro	măzos
	I-ask-FUT	*you-from*	*yours-for,*	*that*	*happy*	*you-seem*

PV	tu	te	des	vudžile	la	mange,	Stevàne.
EB	TU	TE	DES	VUZHILE	LA	MANGE,	STEVANE.
IS	Tu	te	des	vuʒile	la	manqe,	Stev!ane.
	you	*that*	*you-give*	*loan*	*it*	*me-to,*	*Stèvo-VOC.*

"I don't know where my father's shears are, but I'll ask you for yours, because you seem happy to lend them to me, Stèvo."

Miscellaneous Notes on Pronunciation

a) The aspirated sounds <kh>, <ph> and <th> lose their aspiration when they are in final position in a word, thus **jakh** "eye" sounds like [jak] (but *cf.* **jakha** [jakha], "eyes"). No word can contain more than one aspirated stop, thus **khetane(s)** or **kethane(s)** "together," but never *[khethane(s)].

b) The voiced sounds <b>, <d>, <dj>, <dž>, <g>, <v> and <z> are devoiced in word final position, becoming <p>, <t>, <č>, <čh>, <k>, <f> and <s>. Thus **pandž** "five" sounds like [panş], but [panʒḙ] (**pandžḙ**) in the oblique case.

c) Word final consonant clusters lose the last consonant, thus **baxt** "luck" sounds like [bax], **bust** "roasting spit," sounds like [bus], **vast** "hand" sounds like [vas], **čamb** "scalp" sounds like [čam], **brišind** "rain" sounds like [brišin] and so on. The cluster is retained when not word final, thus **baxtalo** "lucky," **busta** "skewers," **brišindalo** "rainy," &c.

d) Final <s> and <š> tend to become voiced if an <l>, <m> or <n> or a voiced consonant begins the following word. Thus **des mangę** "you give me" sounds like [dez mangə], **deš mìji** "ten thousand" like [dež miː], &c.

e) Some speakers pronounce a <s> as <š>, thus **šaj** "able," **našti** "unable," **šel** "hundred,"**šukar** "beautiful," &c., will sound like [saj], [nasti], [sel], [sukar], and so on.

f) In eastern Kalderash particularly, <s> is elided, or becomes an [h] before a following <k> (the initial sound in various grammatical morphemes). Thus [lehko] for **lesko** "his," [merimahki] for **merimaski** "death." The <s> of **si** "is/are" can become lost when it follows a word, thus [šukar i] for **šukar si** "it is beautiful," [so i baro]! for **so si baro!** "how big (it is)!" This is sometimes written with an apostrophe: **šukar 'i, so'i baro**. In Lovari Vlax, the final <s> in the nominalizing suffix {-mos} is frequently dropped: **pharimo'** "weight" (for **pharimos**).

g) Historic /s/ has been lost entirely from the athematic masculine singular subject suffix {-os} in all of the Vlax dialects, thus **fòro** "city," **pètalo** "horseshoe," **lokàlo** "dancehall" (non-Vlax **fòros**, &c.).

h) An <l> at the beginning of a word can sound like an [n] if the preceding word ends in a nasal consonant ([n] or [m]). Examples are [dem neskə] for **dem leskę** "I gave (it to) him," and [arakhljam na] for **arakhljam la** "we found her."

i) An <n> between <a> and <e> (or <i>) can disappear, or become a glide ([j]); thus **Rromani** "Gypsy" can sound like [ʀomaji], **dženja** "ladies" like [ʐeja], **sani** "thin" like [saji] (but **sano**), and so on. For some words, the elided form is now the only form in the dialect, *e.g.* **paj** "water," **kuji** "elbow," **xajing** "fountain; well." <n> may also get dropped from certain personal pronouns (see page 62).

j) Historical /n/ has been lost entirely from the athematic past participle suffix {-men} in all of the Vlax dialects: **rimome** "destroyed," **gonime** "banished" (non-Vlax **gonimen**, &c.).

k) Vlax Romani contracts words extensively, and such elided forms need to be learned individually. Some common ones include **kethane(s)** "together" (from **jekhe** + **than** + **-es**, though this is mainly a European Vlax word; the American Vlax equivalent, also found in Europe, is **and'ekh than**); **m'eg dàta** "once more" (from **maj + jekh + dàta**); **mjal** for **mjazol** "he resembles," **kol** "these" for **kakale** (&c.); **kajtji** and **katji** "so" for **kaditji**, **p'es** and **p'el** "you drink," "he drinks" for **pijes, pijel**; **'star** "why" for **sostar**, and **a'l** and **a'n** "he comes," "they come" for **avel, aven**. Some forms of the definite article are also elided; see page 57.

l) In future tenses formed with an enclitic final {-a} (see page 99), the vowel in the third person suffix is elided in the speech of some individuals. This is accompanied by a shift of stress onto the preceding syllable, thus **àv'la** "he will come" (for **avèla**), **aràkh'na** "they will find" (for **arakhèna**), and so on.

m) Some dialects acquire a non-historic final <-k> on some words, thus **akanak** "now," **naštik** "cannot," **čhurik** "knife" (for **akana, našti, čhuri**).

n) Before present tense suffixes, unstressed <ę> before <r> is dropped from the verb root where it exists, but it is retained in the aorist stem (see page 88). Thus √**putęr-** "open, untie" **putęrdem** "I opened," but **putrav** "I open." Syllabic <l> behaves similarly: **džukęl** "dog," **džukle** "dogs."

o) Before words beginning with a stop consonant, such as <t>, <d> or <dj>, or before <dž>, final <-v> can sound like [p]. Although this is especially characteristic of the Sinti dialects, which are not Vlax, it is also found in some varieties of Vlax as well, especially in Romania. Thus [šop zene] for **šov džene** "six people," [kamap te zav] for **kamav te džav** "I want to go."

p) Eastern Kalderash speakers in particular tend to diphthongize <a> to [aj] in their pronunciation of some words. Examples are [gajzo] for **gadžo** "non-Rom," [bajgi] for **bàgi** "so-called, supposedly," [khajlo] for **khalo** "sated, lazy, full," [pajnz] for **pandž** "five," [čumidajno] for **čumidàno** "trunk, box," [xajsarel] for **xasarel** "he loses," and [pajtjiv] for **patjiv** "honor, respect".

q) Some speakers pronounce a few words which have an historical <e> as [o], thus **voš** "forest, **šoro** "head," **šolo** "rope," **jokhvar** "once," **golo** "he went," **pokelime** "defiled," **tordjol** "he stops" (for **veš, šero, šelo, jekhvar, gelo, pekelime** and **terdjol**). *Cf.* also **so'l duj** for **sa l(e) duj** "both."

r) In eastern Kalderash, the final vowel in such words as **mange, tuke, čhavorrenge**, &c., is neutralized to a schwa [ə], which then sometimes gets written as an <a> (**manga, tuka, čhavorrenga,** &c.). In Machvano Vlax, the same final vowel is raised (page 50).

s) In some Romanian Vlax dialects, the words √**phabar-** "burn," **tatimos** "heat" and √**arakh-** "find" have the forms √**thabar-, takimos** and √**araph-**.

t) In South American Vlax, due to interference from Spanish, [b] and [v] interchange in some words, for example [botraba] for **votràva** "poison" or [balta] for **vàlta** "swamp." In the same dialects, [s] frequently substitutes for [š], this [vis] ~ [bis] for **biš** "twenty." Note also the common pronunciation [lulundʒi] for **luludji** "flower."

u) The front and back high vowels [i] and [u] are interchangeable in some words. Thus **bisterav** ~ **busterav** "I forget," **Zìdovo** ~ **Žùdovo** "Jew," **mir(r)o** ~ **mur(r)o** "my, mine," &c. The vowels in some adoptions from Romanian alternate with their original values: **gindiv** ~ **gundiv** ~ **gindiv** "I think" (< Romanian *gîndi*).

v) Vowels are sometimes inserted into words, thus [kuruva] for **kùrva** "whore," [kirivo] for **kirvo** "godfather."

w) The alveo-dental sounds [r], [l], [n] and [d] alternate or disappear in some pronunciations:

[časulja] for **čàsurja** "hours."
[gundulja] for **gùndurja** "thoughts."
[gurumlja] for **guruvnja** "cows."
[huteri] for **hutèli** "restaurant" (< *hotel*)
[kolkoʁo] for **kòrkorro** "alone."
[kolompidia] for **kolompìrja** "potatoes."
[listoranto] for **ristorànto** "restaurant"
[parpale] for **pàlpale** "back again."
[ʁusuja] for **Rrùsurja** "Russian Vlax Roma."
[ʒandalia] for **žandàrja** "policemen."

x) The transposition of consonants is common in Romani. The following metathesized forms frequently occur:

[amran] for **arman** "curse."
[brek] for **berk** "breast."
[brišin] for **bɛršind** "rain."
[dukhum] for **dumukh** "fist."
[epkaš] for **ekhpaš** "a half."

[fruka] for **fùrka** "fork."
[gurko] for **Grùko** "Greek Rom."
[kivro] for **kirvo** "godfather."
[kretintsa] for **ketrìnca** "apron."
[luduvime] for **luvudime** "esteemed."
[maʁno] for **manrro** "bread."
[potriva] for **protìva** "against"
[prasika] for **pèrsika** "peach."
[rila] for **lìra** "fifty dollars."
[vudar] for **dùvar** "twice."
[vudron] for **vurdon** "wagon."

Notes on Machvano Vlax

Machvano Vlax (*MV*), called *Mačvànska* by its own speakers and *Mačvanìcka* by speakers of Kalderash, is widely spoken in North and South America, and in Australia, the Machvaya having left Europe for those places in the early years of the 20th century. It is not well represented in Europe, however, since many of its speakers were murdered during the Second World War. Machvano Vlax is similar to western Kalderash, and that of the *Serbaya*. The Machvaya trace their migration from the Romani district in Mačva, a town in eastern Serbia.

It differs from Russian Kalderash (*RK*), which is the most widely spoken dialect in the United States, in pronunciation and lexicon in particular; the most characteristic phonological differences include:

a) The sound /dj/ corresponds to *RK* /g/ in certain positions, in particular before /e/ and /i/: *MV* **stadji, djìpsi** *RK* **stagi, gìpsi** "hat;" "Romanichal."

b) *MV* /tj/ in the same environment corresponds to *RK* /k/: *MV* **butji, tjiro** *RK* **buki, kiro** "work;" "your."

c) Final /e/ is raised to /i/ in the pronominal forms [mandji] (for **mange**) "to/for me," [tuči] (for **tuke**) "to/for you," [leši] (for **leske**) "to/for him," &c. This raising, which also affects the back vowels (*ex.* [putjin-], [zuralo] for √**potjin-, zoralo** "pay;" "strong") is most characteristic of the dialects in the Balkan group, spoken in

Bulgaria and parts of eastern Macedonia. *Cf.* also *MV* [mandjis i t'aš]? for **manges i t'aves?** "do you want to come too?"

d) Si "is/are" is pronounced [si], and not [sə] as in *RK*.

e) In *MV* and in Western Kalderash, the final <s> of the adverbializing suffix and the second person singular present tense ending (both {-es}) is often dropped: **tu džane'?** "do you know?," **baxtale'** "luckily" (for **tu džanes?** and **baxtales**).

f) Intervocalic <v> disappears in *MV*, thus [slaː] for **slàva**, "saint's day feast," [soau] for **sovav** "I'm sleeping," [ail] for **avel** "he's coming," [ailem] for **avilem** "I came," &c.

g) Aspirated /th/ can become [č] or [ts] (here <c>), thus [čem] or [tsem] for **them** "country," [koče] or [kotse] for **kothe** "there," &c. The same feature is found in some Romanian Romani dialects.

h) Stress and intonation differ from those in *RK*. In stress-final disyllabic items, there is lengthening of the first syllable and a more even distribution of stress (see next).

i) The retroflex sounds [ş] and [ʐ] (here <čh> and <dž>), which can lose this feature among *RK* speakers, are articulated even more strongly in Machvano Vlax, becoming retroflex [ţ] + [r] and [d] + [r]. Thus **gadžo** "non-Rom" may sound like [gaḓro]. The expression **lačho mačho** "good fish," pronounced [laːţr'o maːţr'o] is imitated by *RK* speakers who regard it as a Machvano shibboleth. The impressionistic representation of the word **džuvli** "woman" in a letter written by a speaker of American Machvano Vlax was <drulie>.

j) Plurals of athematic feminine singular nouns in {-a} are made with {-e} in *MV*, rather than {-i} which is the plural in *RK*. Examples include *MV* **glàte** "children," **bède** "troubles," (*RK* **glàti**, **bèdi**). Note also *MV* **kalderàši**, "Kalderash Roma," (*RK* **kęlḍeràša**).

k) Like the Northern and Central Romani dialects, but unlike Eastern Kalderash, *MV* allows the invariable pronominal forms **amen** ("we/us") and **tumen** ("you") for both subject and oblique cases (*RK* subj. **ame**, obl. **amen**, subj. **tume**, obl. **tumen**).

l) *MV* and *RK* speakers in the United States have a passive knowledge of each others' vocabularies. Differences occur where *MV* has adopted items since their move westwards, sometimes from, or via, Serbian, while *RK* has adopted items from the eastern Slavic languages. Some of the commoner lexical differences include:

Machvanska	Kelderashitska	English
atòska	atùnči	then
atàli	sinìja	table
bizorengo	angl'e zòri	before dawn
blìnče	blìni	crepes
buludjèri	pastùxo	shepherd
cepèlja	cokòlja	shoes
če fàjda?	če hàzna?	what's the use?
čupèrka	burjàca	mushroom
dumùzo	vupòrno	stubborn
fàjda	pučèrja	profit
gadžuno	gadžikano	non-Romani (adj.)
glùpa	than	couch
glùpa	divàno	council
krapivàra	tjèrbo	deer
krišàko	žandàri	policeman
kic-o-	amsuč-i-	twirl the mustache
kropòdo	kuštjàrja	lavatory
lèdo	pàho	ice
loràndja	arànxa	orange
mèklja	matòra	broom
mìko	vitjàzo	giant
nẹrgasto	pùrpura	purple
okòlo	krujal	around
patàvo[1]	ponjàva	carpet
pendjèra	filjàstra	window
rad-i-	munč-i-	strive, labor
ràdka	ràdica	radish
sahàto	čas(orr)o	wristwatch
šùlica	pikùco	arrow
rèzo	horèzo	rice
sestèri	firìzo	saw
svedòko	màrturo	witness

---

[1]The word **patav** in its original meaning (preserved in other dialects) refers to a cloth strip wound around the ankles and feet before putting on one's boots.

šàri	diklo	shawl
tutùnja, tutunìca	sigàra	cigarette
vàdji, još	hìnka	still, yet
vìnte	lìmpunz, frèni	brakes
vulùška	frùka	fork

Lost Words and New Words

Several words which are common in European Vlax became lost in the migration to America. Among these are **kethanes** "together," **valin** "bottle," **kazom** "how many," **ambòrim** "perhaps" and **amal** "friend." In American Vlax these have been replaced by **and'ekh than, bàdla, sòde, dikhàsa** (or **šaj àla**) and **frèno**, some of which are alternative European Romani forms. The arrival of large numbers of Vlax-speaking *themenge Rroma* or Romani emigrants from Europe is reintroducing some of these lost forms. A number of other items also seem to be disappearing from the language, and are being replaced by English-derived words, for example **vrjàmja** "time," √**ažut-i-** "help," and **nùma** "but" (now increasingly **thàjmo**, √**help-i-** and **bęt**). Innovations include **hutèri** "restaurant" (from "hotel"), **àjso** "icecube" (as opposed to **pàho** "ice") and **djùso** "orange juice" (as opposed to **sòko**, "juice"). **Sàto** "important man" is from "(big)shot," and has the feminine form **šatàjka** (*i.e.* "big shot's wife," rather than "important woman"). The word √**prič-o-** "talk, chat," which has been incorporated into Kalderash Romani, is said to be a neologism from "preach," via the born again Christian movement, but this is probably folk etymology, and represents convergence with the already-existing Machvano item which originates in Serbian *pričati* "relate, tell, narrate." Some older Machvaya in the United States have some knowledge of Serbian.

Thematic and Athematic Grammar

Vlax Romani grammar may be treated in two categories: *Thematic* and *Athematic*. These have different historical origins, and different surface morphology. Thematic grammatical rules apply to words in the original stock, *i.e.* words of Indian origin, as well as to words acquired from all other languages the ancestors of the Roma met on the journey westwards before reaching Europe. These include items from Persian, Kurdish, Ossetian, Armenian, Georgian and Byzantine Greek, among others. Athematic grammatical rules apply to words acquired from other languages after crossing into Europe, including later Greek, South Slavic, Romanian, East Slavic, Hungarian, German, English and so on. It is their athematic lexicons which present the principal barrier to mutual intelligibility among the speakers of the different Romani dialects.

Thematic items are almost always stressed on their final syllable, and athematic items almost always on other syllables, thus **šukàr** thematic, and **mùndro**, athematic, which both mean "beautiful." Neither final stress not predictable stress (*i.e.* stress retained on the root or stem of the word) is consistently indicated in this description. If the stress on a word is *not* final or predictable, it is marked with a grave accent (`) as a guide to pronunciation (see page 36); there is some indication that categorization of an item as either thematic or athematic may also be determined by stress placement (see page 116).

Root *vs.* Stem

In this description, *root* is used to refer to the unanalysable base of any word, to which other enclitics may be joined. For example, √dikh- "see." *Stem* refers to the form of a word derived in some way from its root, usually by the addition of an affix or affixes, but which is still not a complete word in itself, and which still requires additional bound morphemes; for example **dikhl-** "saw." An affix such as this {-*l*-} in /**dikh-l-**/, which requires further endings to complete the word, (*e.g.* **dikh-l-em** "I saw"), is here called a *non-final affix*, abbreviated throughout as *NFA*.

Nouns

All nouns belong to one of two grammatical classes or genders, *viz.* masculine and feminine, and they are either singular or plural. They also have three separate cases, depending upon whether they are functioning as the subject of a sentence, the object of a sentence, or are being addressed directly. The subject case is sometimes called the nominative or direct case, the object case is sometimes called the oblique or accusative case (the term *oblique* is used here), and when a noun is the focus of direct address, *e.g.* "hey stupid!," "hey, lady!," "mister!," "Mary!," it is in the vocative case. The gender, number and case of each noun in a sentence must be matched by all the other words which go with it in the nominal group, that is, the articles, the adjectives and the possessives.

Articles

In Romani, as in English, articles are either indefinite (indicated by *a, an* or *some* in English), or definite (indicated by *the* in English). In Romani, but unlike in English, proper nouns as well as common nouns take a definite article, thus **e Marìja** "(the) Mary," **o Parìzo** "(the) Paris." Body parts and illnesses also take definite articles: **dukhal ma o šero** "my [*lit.* "the"] head aches," **ljaspe e sfìnka** "she got (the) mumps."

The indefinite article is the same as the numeral "one," and is marked for the oblique case. In the oblique case, it is also marked for gender. Numeral *one* usually has the form **jekh**, especially when counting, though it has the common alternative form **ekh**. This **ekh** (or even **'kh**, and **eg**[1] before voiced consonants) is used when it is functioning as the indefinite article: **jekh manuš** "one man," **ekh manuš, 'kh manuš** "a man," **eg dori** "a string." Even when used as an article, **ekh** conveys more the sense of "a certain" than its English equivalent, and is usually omitted altogether: **dikhlem džukles avri** "I saw a dog outside."

---

[1]This spelling is not common, but *cf.* **m'eg dàta** "once more."

Articles: Indefinite

	Masculine	*Feminine*
Subject	**ekh rakl-o**	**ekh rakl-i**
Oblique	**ekh-e rakl-es**	**ekh-a rakl-ja**

The indefinite plural "some" is expressed by different words in different Vlax dialects. The most common is **vùni** (or **ùni**), which is invariable, *i.e.* it does not change for gender or case: **vùni rakle(n)** "some boys," **vùni raklja(n)** "some girls." The words **nìšte** (variant **mèšte**) and **vàresode** (or **vàresodja**) are used in the sense of "whatever, some ~ or other:" **nìšte hertìja** "some document or other." The other use of "some," *i.e.* in the sense of "a portion of" ("he ate some cake") is expressed by different words meaning "portion" or "a little bit of:" **'kh cerra, 'kh xànci, 'kh xàri, 'kh kotorro, d'abìja: 'kh cerra manrro** "some bread."

The negative of "there is some" or "there are some," *i.e.* "there isn't any" or "there aren't any," is **ma naj** or **ma naj kak** plus the noun: **ma naj kak zàrro** "there's no sugar." The past tense of this is expressed with **ma nas (kak): ma nas zàrro** "there wasn't any sugar." In Western Vlax, the modifiable word **nisavo** occurs with the negated verb phrase: **naj ma nisave love** "I have no money."

Forms of the Definite Articles and Thematic Nouns

Root: √**rakl**- "(non-Gypsy) child."

When a noun phrase (here, an article and a noun together) is masculine singular, and is the subject of a sentence, it has the form **o raklo** "the boy."

When a masculine singular noun phrase is the object of a sentence, *i.e.* is in the oblique case, it has the form **le rakles** "the boy."

When the singular noun is addressed directly, *i.e.* is in the vocative case, it has the form **rakleja** "(hey) boy!." The thematic stress placement is maintained, since thematic root stress does not shift onto thematic bound morphology: **raklèja**. Articles do not accompany nouns when they are in the vocative case.

When a noun phrase is masculine plural and is the subject of a sentence, it has the form **le rakle** "the boys."

When a noun phrase is masculine plural and is the object of a sentence, it has the form **le raklen** "the boys."

When a plural masculine noun is the object of direct address, it has the form **raklale** (*i.e.* **raklàle**) "(hey) boys!"

When a noun phrase is feminine singular and is the subject of a sentence, it has the form **e rakli** "the girl."

When a feminine singular noun phrase is the object of a sentence, it has the form **la raklja** "the girl."

When a feminine singular noun phrase is the object of direct address, it has the form **raklijo** "(hey) girl!"

When a noun phrase is feminine plural and is the subject of a sentence, it has the form **le raklja** "the girls."

When a noun phrase is feminine plural and is in the oblique case, it has the form **le rakljan** "the girls."

When a plural feminine noun is the focus of direct address, it has the form **rakljale** "(hey) girls!"

The forms <**raklja**>, <**rakljan**> and <**rakljale**> are re-spellings of **rakli-a**, **rakli-an** and **rakli-ale**.

The definite article **le** has the very common alternative form '**e**, written <**e**>. Also for some speakers are the further alternative forms **el**, **ol** and **o'**, especially in dialects spoken in Romania.

The feminine singular definite article **e** has the form **i** in some Vlax (and nearly all non-Vlax) dialects; in Kalderash spoken in Russia, it can have the pronunciation [ə]. Its singular oblique form **la** has the alternative '**a** in some varieties of Lovari.

The root √**rakl-** is called "open" or a "bound" because it has no independent existence, requiring addition bound morphology for all its forms. Many nouns in Romani are closed (or unbound or free) and can stand alone in the singular, and sometimes plural. These all end in consonants, and their morphology differs slightly from the above in their subject case plurals and in the vocative:

58

	Masculine		Feminine	
	Singular	*Plural*	*Singular*	*Plural*
Subject	o rakl-o o sap	le rakl-es le sap-a	e rakl-i e kat	le rakl-j-a le kat-j-a
Oblique	le rakl-e-s le sap-e-s	le rakl-e-n le sap-e-n	la rakl-j-a la kat-j-a	le rakl-j-a-n le kat-j-a-n
Vocative	rakl-e-(j)a sap-a	rakl-a-le sap-a-le	rakl-i-(j)o kat-o	rakl-j-a-le kat-j-a-le

Figure 5: REGULAR THEMATIC NOMINAL AND DEFINITE ARTICLE FORMS

Masculine consonant-final nouns take an {-a} in the subject plural, thus **o Rrom** "the (Gypsy) man," plural **le Rroma**, or **o sap** "the snake," plural **le sapa**.

Feminine consonant-final nouns take an {-a} or {-ja} in the subject plural, thus **e jakh** "the eye," **le jakha** "the eyes," **e kat** "the scissors," **le katja** "the pairs of scissors."

The singular vocative endings for consonant-final nouns are in the singular, unstressed {-a} or {-e} (masculine) and {-o} (feminine), e.g. **dàde** "father!" (< **dad**), **kàto** "oh scissors!" (< **kat**), and in the plural, {-àle} and {-jàle} respectively: **dadàle!, katjàle!** Note the different stress placement between plural and vocative for such items: **Rromà** "Gypsies," **Rròma** "hey Gypsy," **phralà** "brothers," **phràla** "hey brother!"

There are a number of thematic vocative case forms which do not follow the regular pattern. Thus **dej** "mother" has **de!** or **dèja!** or **dàle!**, **čhav** "boy" has **čhàva!**, **Del** "God" has **Dèvla!**, **kak** "uncle" has **kàko!** and **čhej** "girl" has **čhe!** or **čhèja!**. Irregular athematic vocatives are listed on pages 145-146.

Irregular Thematic Plural and Oblique Forms

Common items, and especially those which are monosyllabic, may optionally have the same plural subject form as their singular subject, thus **Rrom** "Gypsy" or "Gypsies," **džukel** "dog" or "dogs," **berš** "year" or "years," **manuš** "man" or "men."

Roots ending with /-v/ demonstrate various plural forms. **Asav** "mill" is made plural like most consonant-final nouns: **asava**. **Prašav** "rib" and **čhav** "(Gypsy) boy," have the plurals **prasave** "mills" and **čhave** "boys," because these are roots with an historical final /-o/ which has been incorporated into the /-v-/. **Dorjav** "river," although from Persian and therefore ostensibly a thematic item, is treated as athematic in Vlax, and has the plural **dorjàvurja**. This may be the result of its root not having final stress.

The feminine noun **jakh** "eye" has the masculine plural oblique stem **jakhen-** rather than the expected *jakhan-. In some Romani dialects, it is treated as a masculine noun (it is neuter in Sanskrit, and feminine in the neo-Indian languages).

The consonant-final feminine noun **rjat** "night" seems to have the underlying form *__rati__, with forward shift of /i/. Except in the vocative case, **rjàto**, this reasserts itself in inflected forms of the word, thus the plural is **ratja**, the oblique stem is **ratja-**, and the root of the verb "to spend the night" is √**ratjar-**.

Some thematic nominal roots with final /-aj/ form their plurals by dropping the /-j/: **rašaj** "holy man," plural **raša**. Further discussion of /-j/ final nouns is found on page 150.

Rril "fart" has the plural **rra**.

Some thematic nominal roots with final /-n/ have irregular plurals, thus **arman** "curse," plural **armaja**, **asvin** "tear," **asva** "tears," **patrin** "leaf," **patrja** "leaves." For more examples of related irregular plurals, see page 150.

Some nouns have irregular oblique stems. Thus **muj** "face, mouth" has in the singular oblique case **mos-**, **dej** "mother" has **da-**, **raj** "gentleman" has **ras-**, **dji** "belly" has **djas-** (in some dialects; otherwise **djes-**) and so on.

Animate vs. Inanimate nouns

Noun phrases which are the object of transitive verbs retain their subject case form *unless they are animate*, in which case they must be put into their oblique form. An exception to this, for some speakers only, is with body parts, which are treated as animate. If the oblique stem has a suffix or an NFA following it (see page 55), it must *always* take the oblique case ending, whether animate or inanimate:

o **kher si purano; me dikhav** *o* **kher**
"the house is old; I see the house" (inanimate)
o **punrro si melalo; me dikhav** *le* **punrres**
"the foot is dirty; I see the foot" (body part)
o **raklo si xarano; me dikhav** *le* **rakles**
"the boy is smart; I see the boy" (animate)
but
me džav *le* **kher-es-te**
"I am going to the house" (inanimate, with suffixes added)

me kindem les *le* rakl-*es-tar*
"I bought it from the boy" (animate, with suffixes added)

Pronouns

Pronouns are of various kinds. Those dealt with in the following section are *personal, disjunctive, interrogative, relative* and *compound* or *indefinite*. Possessive pronouns are treated as possessive adjectives, and are dealt with later on pages 75-76.

Personal Pronouns

Personal pronouns are the kind that go with verbs. There are both subject and oblique case personal pronouns, depending upon whether they represent the "doer" of the verb, or they stand for the receiver of the action of the verb: "I hit the boy" ("I" is the "doer" of *hit*, and is therefore its subject), "the boy hits me" ("me" is the receiver of *hit*, and therefore its object). Verbs which can take objects are transitive (such as *e.g.* "hit"), and verbs which cannot take objects are intransitive, *e.g.* "glow").

In English, the subject personal pronouns are *I, you* (singular), *he, she, it, we, you* (plural) and *they*. The equivalent object or oblique personal pronouns are *me, you* (singular), *him, her, it, us, you* (plural) and *them*.

In Romani, the subject personal pronouns are **me** "I," **tu** "you" (sg.), **vov** "he," **voj** "she," **ame** "we," **tume** "you" (pl.) and **von** "they."[1] Unlike English, there is no separate word for "it," since every noun that "it" refers to will be either masculine or feminine in Romani, and will therefore take the appropriate masculine (**vov**) or feminine (**voj**) pronoun.

There are a couple of nouns which are also used like personal pronouns. These are **gero** (feminine **geri**), literally "wretched one," a kind of negative-sounding third person, and

---

[1]In some non-Vlax dialects, both northern (Welsh Romani) and southern (Bulgarian and Greek Romani), there is a separate set of emphatic personal pronouns for the first and second singular and plural persons: **màja, tùja, amàja** and **tumàja**. Given their distribution, it is likely that they were present in the original language.

kutàri (feminine **kutarjàsa**) which are used when you want to avoid saying -- or else cannot remember -- the actual name of the individual, like "whatsisname" or "you-know-who." They have been included here rather than with the nouns, because like pronouns, but unlike nouns, they cannot take definite articles.

Some of the oblique personal pronouns have both a long and a short form. All of the forms, subject and oblique, are listed here:

	1s	*2s*	*3sm*	*3sf*	*3smfr*	*1p*	*2p*	*3pmf*	*3pmfr*
Subject	me	tu	vov	voj		ame	tume	von	
Oblique (short)	ma'	tu'	le'	la'	pe'	ame'	tume'	le'	pe'
Oblique (long)	man	tut	les	lat	pes	amen	tumen	len	pen

The apostrophes are not usually written with the short forms of the oblique pronouns.

The **pes/pen** forms are *reflexive*, and mean "himself/herself, themselves;" they cannot occur in the subject case. Some speakers use **pes** for both **pes** and **pen**, while others use **pe(s)** in all singular and **pe(n)** in all plural reflexive constructions, thus **arakhav pe** "I behave myself" (instead of **arakhav ma(n)**). These uses should be avoided. Reflexive pronouns are usually written hyphenated to the verb: **me haljera-ma** "I feel." This is useful to distinguish between {pe} as a preposition and {-pe} as a third person reflexive pronoun: **ramol-pe e hertìja** "he autographs the document," **ramol pe e hertìja** "he writes on the document."

The third person singular oblique long form **lat** (or **lan** in Romania) is very rarely heard.

The third person masculine singular oblique **les** has the alternative forms **'es** and **los** for some speakers.

The subject pronoun **vov** is usually pronounced **vo**. It has the forms [ov] or [jov] in non-Vlax dialects; the feminine **voj** is similarly [oj] or [joj] in the non-Vlax dialects, and **von** is [on] or [jon].

Personal subject pronouns as well as nouns can be used by

themselves to indicate the source of direct speech, in the following way:

"Katar aviljan?," me	"where did you come from?," said I.
"Na puč mandar!," e phuri	"Don't ask me!" said the old lady.
"Či džanav," vov.	"I don't know," he said.

Oblique personal pronouns may either precede or follow the verb, thus **ma(n) dikhel** or **dikhel ma(n)** "she sees me." Both long and short forms may occur together: **dikhel ma man** or **man dikhel ma** "she sees me."

Postpositions (*p.* 66) can *only* be affixed to the long forms of the oblique case pronouns, thus **mandar**, not *madar "from me." Forgetting to form the oblique stems for nouns and pronouns before affixing NFAs and postpositions is one of the commonest mistakes that students make.

Disjunctive Pronouns

Romani also has what are called *disjunctive pronouns*. They occur when the pronominal referent to the object noun in a sentence is used together with that noun object elsewhere in the same sentence, thus
o lil kaj ramosardem les
"the letter which I wrote (it)"
e Rromni kaj (or kas) me dem dùma lasa
"the woman whom I spoke with (her)."

When the disjunctive pronoun is to the right of the noun, it is anaphoric; it can also occur to the left of it, cataphorically, thus
dikhlem les le rakles
"I saw (him) the boy"
astarèsas len le mačhen
"you were catching (them) the fish."

Probably because English doesn't have this feature, it is less common in American Vlax than in the dialects spoken in Europe.

Interrogative Pronouns

	Subject	Oblique
"What"	**so**	**sos-**
"What"	**če**	-
"Who"	**kon**	**kas(-)**
"Which"	**sav-** + ADJ endings	**sav-** + ADJ endings

The pronoun **kon** (besides **kongòdi**) also means "whoever," *e.g.* **kon phenela o čačimos si te thos pesko punrro and'e bakàli** "whoever is about to speak the truth should have one foot in the stirrup." It may also mean "some of them," as in **kon bešen, kon uštjen** "some of them are sitting, and some are standing."

In Russian Kalderash as spoken in Europe, the oblique form **kas** "whom" occurs independently for both singular and plural: **le gadže kas prindžardem len** "the men whom I met," but elsewhere it has been replaced by the general relative pronoun **kaj** and can only occur otherwise as a bound morpheme (**kaske** "for whom," **kasko** "whose," **kasgòdi** "whomever," &c.). In American Vlax the same sentence would be **le gadže kaj prindžardem.**

Relative Pronouns

The main relative pronoun in Vlax is **kaj** (var. **ka**), though **so** "what" and **sav-** "which" may be used in the same way:

o lil kaj bičadem les	"the letter which I sent"
džene ka bešen pàša mande	"people who live near me"
kodja paramìči savi phendjan ma	"that tale you told me"
o mobìli so tràdav	"the car I drive"

Relative constructions involving postpositions with animate objects can be expressed in two ways. First of all by adding the postposition to the long oblique form of the relative pronoun, *i.e.*

kas-, or secondly by using the subject form together with the postposed form of the personal pronoun. Thus "those children with whom he's playing" can be either **kodole čhavorre kaj khelel** *lenca* (*lit.* "those children which he plays *with-them*"), or **kodole čhavorre kasa khelel** (*lit.* "those children *with-whom* he plays"). This second possibility is far less likely to be heard. Similarly, constructions such as **o gono** *savestar* **lem me le bales** "the sack *from-which* I look the pig" are possible, but very rare. More usual would be **o gono kaj lem me le bales** *lestar* "the sack which I took the pig *from-it.*" *Cf.* also **e klìška** *pa savjate* **phendem tuke** "the book I told you about, **o Rrom** *kaske* **me phendem** *ej* "the man I said 'hi' to," **o fòro** *katar* **avilem** "the town I came from."

Compound or Indefinite Pronouns

	Subject	*Oblique*
"Somebody"	**vàrekon**	**varekàs-**
"Nobody"	**kònik, nìkon**	**kanikàs-, nikàs-**
"Something"	**vàreso**	**varesòs-**
"Anything"	**(vare)sogòdi**	**(vare)sos- + -gòdi**
"Nothing"	**khànči**	**khančès-**

The word **khančesko** can be used idiomatically to mean "worthless" in both positive and negative constructions: **kodo khančesko gadžo** "that worthless man," **kodo gadžo naj khančesko** "that man is worthless."

Indefinite pronouns with {-**gòdi**} take their bound morphology on the stem and not on the {-**gòdi**}, thus **maj sasagòdi** (= **sas-sa** + **gòdi**) "with anything else." This suffix is discussed further on page 155.

Postpositions, Adjectival NFAs and Prepositions

Postpositions

Like other Indian languages, Romani has postpositions as well as prepositions. Prepositions are *pre*-posed, *i.e* are placed before the noun or pronoun as in English ("*to* the house," "*for* him"), while postpositions are placed after the noun or pronoun, and are joined to it as a suffix.

There are four real postpositions, which in some grammars of Romani are treated as though they were case endings, and which are given names such as dative, ablative, &c. While it may be useful to keep some of these labels, it is easier to regard Romani as having only three distinct cases, *viz.* subject, oblique and vocative, the oblique case being the one which takes the various post-positions.

Stress placement remains on the oblique stem, and is not shifted to the postposition.

The four postpositions are:

{-ke} "for," "to" This marks the indirect object, and is sometimes called the *dative*. The /k/ is voiced to /g/ (thus {-ge}) when it follows the preceding /-n/ of the plural oblique nominal and pronominal forms.

{-sa} "with" Sometimes called the *instrumental*, this is usually written <-ca> when it follows the preceding /-n/ of the plural oblique nominal and pronominal forms because it is realized phonetically as [tsa]. Because the masculine singular oblique stem already ends in /-s/, this is not written twice.

{-tar} "from," "by" Sometimes called the *ablative* or *elative*, this has the form {-dar} when it follows the preceding /-n/ of the plural oblique nominal and pronominal forms.

{-te} "at" Sometimes called the *locative, prepositional* or *illative* this is used, with some restrictions (see page 73), when the noun or pronoun is used with a preposition. The /t/ is voiced to /d/ (thus {-de}) when it follows the preceding /-n/ of the plural oblique nominal and pronominal forms. There is at least one instance of this preposition being used with an adjective: **pe sigate** "with speed" (< **pe** "on, at, for" + **sigo** "quick(ly)" + -te).

Examples with thematic nouns are as follows:

Masculine

o rakl-o	"the boy" (subj.)	**le rakl-e**	"the boys" (subj.)
le rakl-e-s	"the boy" (obl.)	**le rakl-e-n**	"the boys" (obl.)
le rakl-e-s-ke	"for the boy"	**le rakl-e-n-ge**	"for the boys"
le rakl-e-s-sa	"with the boy"	**le rakl-e-n-sa**	"with the boys"
le rakl-e-s-tar	"from the boy"	**le rakl-e-n-dar**	"from the boys"
le rakl-e-s-te	"at the boy"	**le rakl-e-n-de**	"at the boys"
rakl-e-(j)a	"boy!" (vocative)	**rakl-a-le**	"boys!" (vocative)

Feminine

e rakl-i	"the girl" (subj.)	**le rakl-j-a**	"the girls" (subj.)
la rakl-j-a	"the girl" (obl.)	**le rakl-j-a-n**	"the girls" (obl.)
la rakl-j-a-ke	"for the girl"	**le rakl-j-a-n-ge**	"for the girls"
la rakl-j-a-sa	"with the girl"	**le rakl-j-a-n-sa**	"with the girls"
la rakl-j-a-tar	"from the girl"	**le rakl-j-a-n-dar**	"from the girls"
la rakl-j-a-te	"at the girl"	**le rakl-j-a-n-de**	"at the girls"
rakl-i-(j)o	"girl!" (vocative)	**rakl-j-a-le**	"girls!" (vocative)

	SUBJECT "I"	OBLIQUE "me"	REFLEXIVE "myself"	POSSESSIVE MASC.SG.	POSSESSIVE FEM.SG.	POSSESSIVE M/F PLUR.
Sg. 1	me	ma(n)	ma(n)	murro, m'o	murri, m'i	murre, m'e
Sg. 2	tu	tu(t)	tu(t)	čiro, č'o	čiri, č'i	čire, č'e
Sg. 3m	vov	le(s)	pe(s)	lesko	leski	leske
Sg. 3f	voj	la	pe(s)	lako	laki	lake
Sg. 3 refl.			pe(s)	pesko (pako)	peski (paki)	peske, p'e (pake)
Pl. 1	ame	ame(n)	ame(n)	amaro	amari	amare
Pl. 2	tume	tume(n)	tume(n)	tumaro	tumari	tumare
Pl. 3	von	le(n)	pe(n)	lengo	lengi	lenge
Pl. 3 refl.			pe(n)	pengo	pengi	penge
"who"	kon	kas-	pe(s/n)	kasko	kaski	kaske
"who(m)"		kaj	pe(s/n)	kasko	kaski	kaske
"what"	so	sos-	pe(s/n)	sosko	soski	soske
"which" Sg. m	savo	saves	pe(s)	savesko	saveski	saveske
"which" Sg. f	savi	savja	pe(s)	savjako	savjaki	savjake
"which" Pl. m	save	saven	pe(n)	savengo	savengi	savenge
"which" Pl. f	save	savjan	pe(n)	savjango	savjangi	savjange
"someone" m/f	varekon	varekas	pe(s)	varekasko	varekaski	varekaske
"nobody" m/f	konik	kanikas	pe(s)	kanikasko	kanikaski	kanikaske
"nobody" m/f	nikon	nikas	pe(s)	nikasko	nikaski	nikaske
"everyone" m	sváko	svakones	pe(s)	svakonesko	svakoneski	svakoneske
"everyone" f	sváko	svakonja	pe(s)	svakonjako	svakonjaki	svakonjake
"everyone" m/f	savorre	savorren	pe(s)	savorrengo	savorrengi	savorrenge
"anyone" Sg. m	fersavo	fersaves	pe(s)	fersavesko	fersaveski	fersaveske
"anyone" Sg. f	fersavi	fersavja	pe(s)	fersavjako	fersavjaki	fersavjake
"anyone" Pl. m	fersave	fersaven	pe(n)	fersavengo	fersavengi	fersavenge
"anyone" Pl. f	fersave	fersavja	pe(n)	fersavjango	fersavjangi	fersavjange
"something"	váreso	vareso(s)	pe(s)	varesosko	varesoski	varesoske
"nothing"	khánči	khanči	pe(s)	khančesko	khančeski	khančeske
"anything"	sogódi	sogódi	pe(s)	soskogódi	soskigódi	soskegódi

Figure 6: TABLE OF PRONOMINAL FORMS

POSSESSIVE FEM.SG.OBL.	DATIVE "to/for"	LOCATIVE var.preps.	INSTRUMENTAL "by/with"	ABESSIVE "without"	ABLATIVE "from"
murra, m'a	mange	mande	manca	bi-mango	mandar
čira, č'a	tuke	tute	tusa	bi-tuko	tutar
leska	leske	leste	lesa	bi-lesko	lestar
laka	lake	late	lasa	bi-lako	latar
peska, p'a	peske	peste	pesa	bi-pesko	pestar
(paka)	(pake)	(pate)	(pasa)	(bi-pako)	(patar)
amara	amenge	amende	amenca	bi-amengo	amendar
tumara	tumenge	tumende	tumenca	bi-tumengo	tumendar
lenga	lenge	lende	lenca	bi-lengo	lendar
penga	penge	pende	penca	bi-pengo	pendar
kaska	kaske	kaste	kasa	bi-kasko	kastar
kaska	kaske	kaste	kasa	bi-kasko	kastar
soska	soske	soste	sosa	bi-sosko	sostar
saveska	saveske	saveste	savesa	bi-saveske	savestar
savjaka	savjake	savjate	savjasa	bi-savjake	savjatar
savenga	savenge	savende	savenca	bi-savenge	savendar
savjanga	savjange	savjande	savjanca	bi-savjange	savjandar
varekaska	varekaske	varekaste	varekasa	bi-varekaske	varekastar
kanikaska	kanikaske	kanikaste	kanikasa	bi-kanikaske	kanikastar
nikaska	nikaske	nikaste	nikasa	bi-nikaske	nikastar
svakoneska	svakoneske	svakoneste	svakonesa	bi-svakoneske	svakonestar
svakonjaka	svakonjake	svakonjate	svakonjasa	bi-svakonjaske	svakonjastar
savorrenga	savorrenge	savorrende	savorrenca	bi-savorrenge	savorrendar
fersaveska	fersaveske	fersaveste	fersavesa	bi-fersaveske	fersavestar
fersavjaka	fersavjake	fersavjate	fersavjasa	bi-fersavjake	fersavjatar
fersavenga	fersavenge	fersavende	fersavenca	bi-fersavenge	fersavendar
fersavjanga	fersavjange	fersavjande	fersavjansa	bi-fersavjange	fersavjandar
varesoska	varesoske	varesoste	varesosa	bi-varesoske	varesostar
khančeska	khančeske	khančeste	khančesa	bi-khančeske	khančestar
soskagódi	soskegódi	sostegódi	sosagódi	bi-soskegódi	sostargódi

And some examples with personal pronouns:

me	"I" (subject)	**tu**	"you" (sg. subj.)
man	"me" (oblique)	**tu-t**	"you" (sg. obl.)
man-ge	"to, for me"	**tuṭ-ke**	"to, for you"
man-sa	"with me"	**tuṭ-sa**	"with you"
man-dar	"from, by me"	**tut-tar**	"from, by you"
man-de	"at, to me"	**tut-te**	"at, to you"
la-tar	"from her"	**am-e-n-dar**	"from us"
pe-s-sa	"with him/herself"	**le-n-de**	"to, at them"
tum-e-n-sa	"with you (pl.)"	**pe-n-dar**	"from themselves"

Some of these underlying combinations are shown differently in the Pan-Vlax orthography; in particular, double consonants are reduced to one (<tute>, <pesa>), and /s/ following /n/ is written and pronounced <c>: <manca>, <tumenca>. Oblique marker {t} on the second person singular **tut** disappears before /k/ and /s/ in spelling and in pronunciation: <tuke>, <tusa>.

In some Romanian Vlax, {-sa} "with" has the form {-ja} in the feminine singular: **dželem la rakljaja** "I went with the girl."

Note the difference between the non-reflexive and the reflexive personal pronouns in *e.g.* **pučhle lendar** "they asked them" and **pučhle pendar** "they asked each other," "they asked themselves." Another way of saying "each other" is **von dę von: volisarde von dę von** "they loved each other."

Sometimes confusion may arise because of different interpretations of the same postposition, thus **kindajle le gadžestar** could mean either "they were bought *from* the man" or "they were bought *by* the man." In such cases, sentences like the latter should be rephrased as active, rather than passive, constructions.

Expressions of *Without*: {bi-} and {nà-}

The prefix {*bi-*} expresses "without" when used with nouns and pronouns, and "un-" when used with adjectives. Nominal combinations with this prefix are called *abessive*, or sometimes *privative*. It cannot be attached to nouns, with one exception, *viz.*

the word **bìbaxt** "misfortune" (< **baxt** "luck").

With adjectives, such contrastive pairs as **pharo** "heavy" and **bipharo** "light," or **londo** "salty," **bilondo** "insipid, spineless (fig.)," and their derived adverbial forms (page 104) **biphares** "lightly," **bilondes** "spinelessly" are common. Adjectival forms which may also take {**bi-**} include vebal past participles, *e.g.* **bihuladi** "dishevilled," **bimeretime** "unmarried."

With nouns and pronouns, this prefix must operate with the adjectival suffixes, and *not* with the instrumental {**-sa**}, thus **ekh bistadjako raklo** "a hatless boy," **ekh bilovengi džuvli** "a penniless woman." Note also the special forms compounded with this for the personal pronouns: **bi-mango, bi-tumengo,** &c., listed in full on pages 68-69. The word **bi** may also operate as an independent word, thus **bi murri rovli** "without my stick."

The stressed prefix {**nà-**} is common in eastern Vlax dialects in Europe, but has not survived in American Vlax. It has a more restricted use than {**bi-**}, meaning something like "un-": **nàvučo** "low," **nàšukar** "plain," **nàlačho** "bad."

Noun-plus-Noun Genitives

Genitive constructions consisting of two nouns, where the first is usually a container or a measurement, or is the word for "kind" or "sort," are not inflected:

ekh taxtaj čàjo	"a glass of tea"
trin fu(r)tàrja čàso	"three quarters of an hour"
kodja piri zumi	"that dish of soup"
dešujekh ìnči sùrma	"eleven inches of wire"
ekh bari karàfa mol	"a large flagon of wine"
pandž kučja kàfa	"five cups of coffee"
ekh bužo lon	"a bag of salt"
ekh gono kolompìrja	"a sack of potatoes"
če fjàlo klìška sas?	"what kind of book was it?"

This last example, which uses the athematic noun **fjàlo** (from Romanian *fel*), may also be expressed thematically using forms of **so** "what" or **sav-** "which:" **soski klìška sas? savjaki klìška sas?**

The Adjectival NFA

Often treated as a postposition is the adjectival NFA {-k-}, but unlike the postpositions this is marked for gender, number and case in the same way as ordinary adjectives (page 74). Like postpositions, its consonant is voiced (thus becoming {-g-}) when it follows a preceding nominal or pronominal stem ending with /-n/; also like the postpositions, it may only be affixed to the oblique stem. Besides functioning adjectivally, it is also used to create the possessive or *genitive* form of a noun or third-person pronoun, both singular and plural (first and second person pronouns have their own possessive forms — see page 75).

le rakl-e-s-k-o mobìli	"the boy's car"
le rakl-e-n-g-o mobìli	"the boys' car"
le rakl-e-s-k-e mobìlja	"the boy's cars"
le rakl-e-n-g-e mobìlja	"the boys' cars"
la rakl-j-a-k-o mobìli	"the girl's car"
le rakl-j-a-n-g-o mobìli	"the girls' car"
la rakl-j-a-k-e mobìlja	"the girl's cars"
le rakl-j-a-n-g-e mobìlja	"the girls' cars"
le rakl-e-s-k-e mobilèstar	"from the boy's car"
la rakl-j-a-k-a piškirjasa	"with the girl's towel"
murra phej-a-k-a rovljasa	"with my sister's stick"
tumare amal-e-s-k-i raxàmi	"your friend's coat"

In English, constructions of the type "a glass container" are ambiguous, since it is not clear whether the container is to hold glass or else is made of glass. In Romani, the difference is indicated by employing either the dative postposition: **ekh stiklake làda** "a container for glass," literally "a glass's container," or the appropriate adjectival suffix: **ekh stiklaki làda** "a (made of) glass container," literally "a glass-ADJ container." *Cf.* also the possible syntactic order **ekh làda stiklake, ekh làda stiklaki.**

In other Romani dialects, and residually in Vlax (see page

143), the adjectival NFA is {-kr-} ({-gr-}) or {-ker-} ({-ger-}): **le raklesk(e)ro mobìli** "the boy's car," **leng(e)ro mobìlja** "their cars."

Prepositions

Nouns and pronouns which follow prepositions take the locative suffix, but not when a definite article appears in the phrase. Thus **pàša mande** "near me," **maškar amende** "amongst ourselves," **maškar bešimatande** "between sessions," **ànda ekhe bare vešeste** "from a big forest," but *cf.* **ande o veš**, and *not* ***ande le vešeste** "in the forest," because of the coocurrence of the definite article. In ordinary speech, this locative postposition is often not used with nouns whatever the construction, although it is always used with personal pronouns.

The Romani prepositions include:

agora	"from the end of"	**pa**	"concerning," through"
ànda	"from," "by"	**pàla**	"behind," "after"
ande, an'	"in"	**pàša**	"near"
àngla	"in front of"	**pe**	"on," "for (a price)"
avrjal pa	"outside (of)"	**perdal**	"across"
dži ande	"up to"	**pìne**	"until"
dži ka	"up to," "until"	**potrìva**	"against"
intjal	"across"	**prečiv**	"against"
ka	"to"	**rròta**	"around"
karing	"towards"	**sar**	"like," "as"
kàta	"from," "by"	**sìsta**	"near"
kàtar	"from," "by"	**trujal**	"around" (also **krujal**)
krugom	"around"	**tèla**	"under," "beneath"
maškar	"between," "among"	**vaš**	"for"
opral pa	"over"	**vi**	"also"

The meanings listed here are only the primary glosses for these prepositions; further uses for each one are often idiomatic, and must be learned individually. Thus **pe** means "on" (**thodja pesko taxtaj pe e sinìja** "he put his glass on the table") but can also mean "for," both with amounts and with periods of time: **sòde**

pučhes pe late "how much are you asking for it?," **pe sorro djes** "for the entire day."

Prepositions very commonly contract with other words, especially with articles. Such contractions should be indicated in print by an apostrophe. Thus **p'ekh čàso** "for an hour," **pàš'amende** "near us," **an'amaro kher** "in our house." Note the difference between **ànd'e** "from the" (< **ànda e**) and **and'e** "in the" (<**ande e**), and the difference between **kàtar** "from," a preposition, and **katar** (*i.e.* **katàr**) "where from?," an adverb: **me pučhlem le raklestar kàtar o gav katar kindjas pesko mobìli** "I asked the boy from the village where he bought his car from."

Sar and **vi** behave as prepositions even though they are conjunctions and adverbs (*cf.* English "like unto"), and nouns and pronouns following them should take the locative suffix, thus **sar mande** "like me," **vi tute** "you too."

In Kalderash Vlax as spoken in Russia, **kàta** "by," "from," "past," and **ka** "to," "near," cannot be used with feminine singular nouns; **kataj** and **kaj** are used instead. Elsewhere, **kàtar** and **ka** respectively are used for all nominal forms. The preposition **ka** may also be used in possessive constructions (discussed at 86*d*).

"Instead of" is expressed with **so** ("what") or **ànda** ("from"): **so sas t'avel khere, o Rrom teljardja** "instead of coming home, the man left," **me kindem o xabe, ànda murre phejate** "I bought the food instead of my sister (buying it)."

The preposition **vaš**, although a native item (< Sanskrit *vāś* "by means of"), is found in several dialect groups but has generally become lost in Vlax. It survives in the eastern Kalderash spoken in Europe, however: **but zor vaš tumari butji** "much power to your effort." In other dialects, though not in Vlax, the related **vàše** "for that reason," "because of that," also survives from the original Romani (*cf.* Prakrit *vāśa* "on account of").

Adjectives

Adjectives must take the appropriate endings to match the gender, number and case of the nouns they accompany. These are as follows, using **o baro raklo** "the big boy" as a model:

	Masculine	*Feminine*
Sing. subject	o bar-o rakl-o	e bar-i rakl-i
Sing. oblique	le bar-e rakl-e-s	la bar-j-a rakl-j-a
Plur. subject	le bar-e rakl-e	la bar-e rakl-j-a
Plur. oblique	le bar-e rakl-e-n	le bar-e rakl-j-a-n

Adjectives may follow, as well as go before, the nouns they describe, so that **o raklo baro**, &c., is possible. Placement of the adjective, *i.e.* before or after the noun, is conditioned by style or emphasis. The latter in particular may be expressed by repeating the definite article with a post-nominal adjective, thus **o raklo o baro**, meaning something like "the boy, the big (one)." This operates adjectivally, but makes use of the nominal function of adjectives (as in *e.g.* French or German or Spanish), where they may occur independently with an article, thus: **o baro** "the big one," **e šukar** "the beautiful one," **le dile** "the foolish ones." When they follow the noun in this way, all of the nominal morphology is copied onto the adjective as well, *e.g.* **le raklesa le baresa** "with the big boy" (discussed further on page 142).

Adjectives which are derived from nouns by the addition of the NFA {-k-}, *e.g.* **nakhesk-** "nosed" (< **nakh** "nose") or **bukak-** "cheeked" (< **bùka**, "cheek"), and which are themselves modified by another adjective, take the invariable ending {-e}, thus **bare nakhesko raklo** "(a) big-nosed boy," **lole bukaki rakli** "(a) red-cheeked girl" (and not *lolja bukaki rakli). Adjectives otherwise derived from nouns are dealt with on pages 152*ff*.

Possessive Adjectives

Possessive pronouns ("my," "your," &c.) are in fact adjectives, and share the same endings with adjectives. The roots of the personal possessive pronouns, with variant pronunciations, are as follows:

murr- "my" (also **munrr-, mundr-, murr-, morr-, mir(r)-**)
tjir- "your," sg. (also **čir-, kir-**)
les-k- "his" (also **lehk-**)
la-k- "her"
pes-k- "his own," "her own," "its own" (also **peh-k-**)
amar- "our"
tumar- "your" pl.
len-g- "their"
pen-g- "their own"

These may also function as possessive absolute nouns, *i.e.* to mean "mine," "yours," "his," "hers," &c. in such constructions as **kado si amaro** "this is ours," **le murri** "take mine," &c. They take all the NFAs and suffixes necessary as nominals: **kerdjas les murresa** "he did it with mine," **vàzde la lengestar** "lift it out of theirs."

Possessive pronouns, like other adjectives, may also follow the noun, and can take the definite article as well: **murro džukel** "my dog," **o murro džukel, o džukel murro,** "my dog (in particular)," **o džukel o murro** "my dog (in particular)," also *cf.* **le džukles le murres** in the oblique case.

Possessive nouns, which also function adjectivally, are discussed on page 72.

Some speakers use the **pes-k-** form for both singular and plural persons, and do not have **pen-g-** in their idiolect. Each should be used appropriately. The rarely-heard forms **pa-k-** "her own" and **pir-** "your (sg.) own" are new possessive pronouns created by analogy with **la-k-** and **pes-k-**.

Some speakers express "own" for the first and second persons with the words **vlàsno** or **čačuno,** thus **murro vlàsno dad** "my own father," **tj'i čačuni phej** "your own sister."

Short Forms of the Possessive Pronouns

The first two singular possessive pronominal adjectives **murr-** and **tjir-** and the singular *own*-form **pes-k-,** also have the commonly abbreviated variants **m'-, tj'-** and **p'-,** thus **m'o džukel** "my dog," **tj'i mùca** "your cat," **p'e phral** "his (or her) own brothers."

Short-forms cannot be used in possessive absolute position, thus **kadja si tjiro** "this is yours," not *****kadja si tj'o**. A possible exception to this may be the vocative **phrala m'o!** "hey brother!," though **m'o** here could be the separate term of address **mo**.

Equative, Comparative and Superlative Adjectives

The equative construction, "*as. . . as*" uses **(de) sar. . . vi**. Although **vi** is an adverb, nouns and pronouns following it are not in the subject case (as in English), but must take the locative postposition (see page 67).

vov si sar baro vi mande "he is as big as I"
vov si de sar baro vi late "he is as big as she"
sar bare sam vi le avre raklende "we're as big as the other boys"

The comparative ("bigger") and the superlative ("biggest") employ the invariable word **maj** "more." **Maj** alone plus the adjective gives the comparative, *e.g.* **maj baro** "bigger," while with the appropriate definite article it translates the superlative: **o maj baro, e maj bari, le maj bare** "the biggest." *Than* is translated either by using the ablative postposition ("from") with the noun or pronoun, or by using the preposition **kàtar**, which also means "from," or **vi**, meaning "also," both followed by the noun or pronoun with the locative postposition:

vov si maj baro tutar "he is bigger than you" (= "from you")
vov si maj baro katar tute "he is bigger than you" (= "from you")
vov si maj baro vi tute "he is bigger than you" (= "also you")
vov si o maj baro "he is the biggest"
voj si e maj bari "she is the biggest"

The word **maj** is an athematic item adopted from Romanian. The thematic comparative and superlative makes use of the suffix {**-der**}, for example **bar-e-der** "bigger," **o bar-e-der** "the biggest," but this has been lost in the Vlax dialects. It survives in one comparative construction only, *viz.* **feder** (or **fededer**) "better," although this only occurs in the combination **maj fe(de)der** with the specialized meaning of "rather," "preferably." In the standardized Romani dialect, thematic comparatives and superlatives are constructed with {**-der**}, and athematic with **maj**.

78

The oppositional construction *"the more. . . the more"* is formed using **ši maj. . . ši maj** (from Romanian), thus

ši maj barili, ši maj džungajli
"the more she grew, the uglier she got"
ši maj gilàbas, ši maj dukhal m'e kan
"the more you sing, the more it hurts my ears"

"Less" is expressed using **maj xanci. . .(de) sar** or **maj xanci . . .vi**, thus

voj si maj xanci susmàvo de sar tute "she's less modest than you"
me sim maj xanci sitjerdo vi late   "I am less educated than she"

The Particles *TE* and *KE*

TE

The Vlax Romani verb has no infinitive[1], and constructions such as "I hope to go" must be expressed with indicative verbs. This is accomplished with the particle **te**, which may be translated in this case as "that," and which is used to link the indicative forms:

nedeždi'-ma vi te džav
"I hope that I go too," (*i.e.* "I hope me also that I go")
kames te kheles
"you like to dance" (*i.e.* "you like that you dance")

The word **te** is also used before a verb to mean something like "may" or "please;" this is sometimes called the *optative* or *hortative* construction. Some examples are:

te prostin tumen o Del	"may God forgive you"
te trajis lungones	"may you live long"
te bešes tele	"please sit down"
te xan tumenge sastimasa	"may you eat in health"

---

[1]The Central dialects have created a new infinitive using the third person plural ending {-en}, so that "I want to sit down," which is **mang*a*v te beš*a*v** in Vlax, is **mangav te bešen**. In the Northern (as well as some Central) dialects, though not in Welsh Romani, an infinitive has been created with the third person singular suffix {-el}: **mangav te bešel**. In Romanian Vlax, infinitives derived from Romanian verbs are marked with what is written <-ju>: **mangel te vorbju** "he wants to talk," which is also the first person singular ending (see Sarău, 1992:63). Phonetically this is the same as [-iv].

Thirdly, **te** is the Romani word for "if" or "whether:" **či džanav te khere lo vaj nìči** "I don't know whether he's home or not," **te na avel, xoljako avav** "if he doesn't come I'll be angry," **vèsolo avav te pàle dikhava tut** "I'll be happy if I see you again" (this last example can also mean "I'll be happy to see you again"). Some Machvano speakers also use the longer form **te àla** for "if."

Fourthly, **te** means "so that" or "to the extent that:" **kadiči delas duma te bisterdja o čàso** "he talked so much that he forgot the time." This has the alternative form **ta**.

Lastly, **te** can mean "in order to," which has the alternative form **kàšte te: sitjilem e francuzìcka (kàšte) te tràdav and'e Fràncija** "I learnt French in order to travel in France."

When **te** joins two verbs and doesn't mean "if," the second verb cannot take the future suffix {-a} (discussed on page 99). It does when it means "if" or "whether," however: **adžukerav leske te aresel** "I'll wait for him to arrive," **adžukerav te džanav te aresela** "I'll wait to see whether he'll arrive."

When the negator **či** follows **te**, is usually becomes **na**, although not all speakers do this: **spidem les te na amboldel** "I urged him not to return," **mangav te na des jekh svàto** "I want you not to say a word" (cf. **či mangav tut te des jekh svàto** "I don't want you to say a word").

Note also: **te na nìči m'o mobìli, àpo kasko?** "if it isn't my car, then whose (is it)?," **te na nič' adjes, kàna?** "if not today, when?".

KĘ

Kę may, like *te*, be used to join verbs, though its use implies a stronger or more definite sentiment than the latter, thus **mangav ke aves manca** "I want you to come with me" has the suggestion of an order or of a real desire, while **mangav te aves manca** is more like a request or a wish. **Ke** may also be used as an emphatic optative, thus **ke stràzo aves** "please come soon," which carries more emphasis that **te stràzo aves**.

Ke is used as a complementizer to introduce sentences embedded in larger sentences, and is best translated in this function by "that." Thus **me džanglem ke khere sanas** "I knew that you were

80

at home." This use contrasts with that of the relativizer **kaj** (page 65):

a) **e bužerìja *ke* phendja ma e Rajìda xoxajmos sas**
b) **e bužerìja *kaj* phendja ma e Rajìda xoxajmos sas**

Both of these mean "the rumor that Rajida told me was a lie," but in (*a*), the lie was that Rajida told me. In (*b*), the lie was the rumor itself.

Ke also means "because:" **rovèlas ke xasardja p'o slàjboko** "she was crying because she lost her purse." Other words for "because" are **vèska** and **fìnka**. Use of "because" for the complementizer "that," both of which are translated by **ke**, is a typical ethnolectal feature of American Romani English: "I heard because he died."

Verbs

Verbs in Romani have two basic tenses, present and aorist, from which other tenses and aspectual forms are derived. Thematic verbal morphology differs from athematic morphology in a number of ways, and is dealt with later in the book.

Vlax Romani verbs have no infinitive form. In English, this is marked by the word *to*; it is the verb with no subject ("to run," "to walk," "to eat," &c.). When the verb does have a subject, ("*I* run," "*you* walk," "*the cow* eats"), it is called the indicative, and all constructions which would have an infinitive in English (*e.g.* "I hope to go") must be constructed with an indicative in Romani (see page 78). Lacking an infinitive, Romani verbs are listed simply as roots, to which NFAs and suffixes are added to show person, number, aspect and tense. It is not necessary for personal pronouns to accompany the verb, but they are used for emphasis or to disambiguate identical forms (for example the second and third persons in the present tense plural, which both take the same suffix {**-en**}).

Note that the verbal suffixes carry the stress of the whole inflected word unless otherwise indicated.

Thematic Present Tense Suffixes

The present tense translates all of the following English constructions: "I see a man in the distance," "I do see a man in the distance," "do I see a man in the distance?," "I see my teacher each week," "I am seeing a specialist." The following endings are the regular thematic set and are added to the root of the verb (here √dikh-, "see," "look"). Irregular thematic endings are discussed on page 94.

me dikh-*av*	"I see"	ame dikh-*as*	"we see"
tu dikh-*es*	"you (sg.) see"	tume dikh-*en*	"you" (pl.) see"
vov dikh-*el*	"he, it sees"	von dikh-*en*	"they see"
voj dikh-*el*	"she, it sees"		

Imperatives

The imperative, or command form of the verb is usually, though not always, simply the root if you are addressing one person, and the root + {-en} if you are addressing more than one person:
dikh! "look!" (to one person)
dikhen! "look!" (to more than one person)
There are a number of irregular thematic imperatives, particularly with verbs not of the above type, discussed below at *p.* 94.

Negatives

A verb is negated by means of the word **či** placed before it:
dikhav "I see"
či dikhav "I don't see"
Some Vlax dialects spoken in parts of Romania, Bulgaria, Macedonia, Serbia, Bosnia and elsewhere use *ni* to negate verbs. Others, in Greece and Bulgaria, use *in*; still others use *na*. Some American Vlax speakers use a double negative marker, *či-ni.*

If the negative accompanies an imperative verb, then it has the form **na**, and never **či*. This can be translated as *don't*:

na dikh, Etelìjo! "don't look, Ethel!" (*i.e.* to one person)

na dikhen, čhavale! "don't look, boys! (to more than one person)

Dialects which use **na** as the non-imperative (that is, general) negative marker, use **ma** instead of **na** for the imperative. This was part of the original Romani grammar, and its loss in the Vlax dialects serves to distinguish them from the non-Vlax dialects. In areas where they are in contact with dialects which use **ma**, speakers of some Vlax dialects have reintroduced it into their own speech.

Adverbs (page 108*ff.*) are negated with **na**, and not with **či**: **me mardem les, 'ma na zorales** "I hit him, but not hard."

The invariable preverbal **mùsaj** "must" is likewise only negated with **na**: **na mùsaj te ačhes** "you mustn't stay."

The Verb *To Be*

This verb behaves differently from all other verbs. Syntactically, it usually comes at the end of the sentence or phrase (**murro mobìli si** "it's my car"). In the present tense, it has the following conjugation:

me sim	"I am"	**ame sam**	"we are"
tu san	"you (sg.) are"	**tume san**	"you (pl.) are"
vov si	"he, it is"	**von si**	"they are"
voj si	"she, it is"	**si**	"there are"
si	"there is"		

In some varieties of European Vlax the second person plural **san** has the separate form **sen**.

Variant pronunciations of forms of the *BE*-verb with an initial *i-* are occasionally heard, thus **isim, isan, isi, isam**, though this feature is more typical of Balkan dialects than of Vlax.

Si is pronounced [hi] or [i] by some speakers of Vlax, particularly in the northern part of Romania and parts of Hungary, although this is far more commonly found in the non-Vlax dialects. This pronunciation is especially common in postnominal position: **baro 'i** "it's big" (for **baro si**). Contracted with **so** "what," thus so'i, it has the idiomatic meaning of "how ~!" thus **so'i šukar!** "how beautiful!."

Noun phrases following forms of *BE* remain in the subject case.

Because **si tu(t)** or **tu(t) si** means "you have" and not "it is you," **tu san** is used to translate this instead. Thus on the telephone, for "it that you?" you must say **tu san?** (and not *tu si?*).

The imperative of *BE* is **av** (**aven** in the plural):

av sasto! "be healthy!" (sg.)

na aven čaplade! "don't be silly! (pl.)

BE need not be expressed in locative constructions, or with adjectives: **kaj e Gèža?** "where is Geža?," **and'e sòba, voj** "she's in the room," **lindrali voj** "she's sleepy," **vàreso othe** "there's something there." *Cf.* also constructions of the kind **lachi tjiri rjat**[1] "good night," **baro lako kher** "her house is big," &c.

Another way to express *BE* in the third person, especially with animate nouns, is by putting the words **lo** (masculine singular), **la** (feminine singular) or **le** (masculine and feminine plural) after the predicate, instead of using **si**:

vov si baro *or* **baro lo** "he's big"

voj si bari *or* **bari la** "she's big"

von si bare *or* **bare le** "they're big"

The noun or pronoun can be used together with this post-posed verb for emphasis, thus **kaj la voj?** "where *is* she?," **kaj lo vov** "where *is* he?," **vov lo dilo** "he's stupid," **voj la šukar!**, "she's beautiful!."

Note also the constructions **naj lo, naj la, naj le**, "there isn't," "there aren't:" **naj lo dženo kaj adžukerel** "there's no person waiting."

The negative of *BE* is constructed with **či** like other verbs, but only in the first and second person singular and plural persons (**me či sim, tume či san**, &c.). The third persons have a separate negative form, which is the **naj** referred to above. This is analysable as negator **na** plus the abbreviated form of **si**, *viz.* **'i** (**na** + **'i** = **naj**). You *cannot* say *či si* or *naj si*, only **naj**, although such combinations are errors commonly made by students.

---

[1]A calque on the Balkan idiom, *e.g.* Greek καλή σου νύκτα, "good your night."

Na, however, can co-occur with **si** for emphasis: **na zoralo si!** "he's *not* powerful!" (for **naj zoralo**). In Balkan, Central and Northern Romani, the equivalent of **naj** is **nàne**, while the equivalent of **si** is **hi** (marked for gender and number in some Central dialects: **hino**, masculine singular, **hini**, feminine singular and **hine**, plural).

Translate **naj** as "he isn't," "she isn't," it isn't," "there isn't (any)" and "there aren't (any)." With nouns, *no* is also expressed by **ma naj (kak)** or **na naj (kak)**: **ma naj kak pràvo** "there's no ammunition," **ma naj ma sigàra** "I have no cigarettes." The past tense of this is **ma nas (kak)** or **na nas (kak)**: **ma nas ma baxt** "I had no luck" (see the following section).

Naj may also be placed in final position: **but baro naj** "it's not very big."

Verbs: Past Tenses: The Imperfect

There are three past tense categories, the aorist, the imperfect and the pluperfect. The simplest one to construct is the imperfect, which is made simply by adding unstressed {**-as**} to each of the present tense forms. It will change *e.g.* "I see" into "I used to see" or "I was seeing:"

dikhav	"I see"	**dikhàvas**	"I used to see; was seeing"
dikhes	"you see"	**dikhèsas**	"you (sg.) used to see, were seeing"
dikhel	"he sees"	**dikhèlas**	"he used to see; was seeing"
dikhas	"we see"	**dikhàsas**	"we used to see; were seeing"
dikhen	"you see"	**dikhènas**	"you (pl.) used to see, were seeing"
dikhen	"you see"	**dikhènas**	"you (pl.) used to see, were seeing"

Stress has been added here only as a guide. Be careful not to say *[dikhavàs], [dikhelàs], &c.

To make the past tense of *BE*, also add {**-as**} to the present tense forms. The third person singular and plural, however, modifies this slightly, *i.e.* to **sas** (and not *sias):

sìmas	"I was"	**sàmas**	"we were"
sànas	"you (sg.) were"	**sànas**	"you (pl.) were"
sas	"he, she, it was"	**sas**	"they were"
sas	"there was"	**sas**	"there were"

The **sas** form has a separate negative **nas** (< **na** + **sas**); all other persons are negated with **či** (**me či sim**, &c.). This may occur in final position: **lačho nas** "it wasn't good."

Verbs: Expressing Possession

a) Nouns and pronouns postpositioned with {-**te**} and {-**ke**} are used to express possession in Romani. These are:

mange	"to, for me"	**mande**	"to, at me"
tuke	"to, for you"	**tute**	"to, at you"
leske	"to, for him"	**leste**	"to, at him"
lake	"to, for her"	**late**	"to, at her"
peske	"to, for him/herself"	**peste**	"to, at him/herself"
amenge	"to, for us"	**amende**	"to, at us"
tumenge	"to, for you"	**tumende**	"to, at you"
lenge	"to, for them"	**lende**	"to, at them"
penge	"to, for themselves"	**pende**	"to, at themselves"

le rakleske	"to, for the boy"	**le rakleste**	"to, at the boy"
le raklenge	"to, for the boys"	**le raklende**	"to, at the boys"

la rakljake	"to, for the girl"	**la rakljate**	"to, at the girl"
le rakljange	"to, for the girls"	**le rakljande**	"to, at the girls"

b) There is no verb "to have" in Romani, although Balkan dialects can use the verb √**ther**- "hold, catch," to mean something like "possess," and some Vlax speakers have adopted this in areas of contact. Possession is regularly indicated, however, by using the third person of the *BE* verb, that is **si**, to be translated as "there is," "there are," used with the above nominal or pronominal forms: **si mande, si le rakleste**. Such combinations then translate as "there is/are to me," "there is/are to the boys," &c., *i.e.* "I have," "the boys have," &c.

c) There is a difference between possessive constructions with {-**ke**} and those with {-**te**}; the first expresses general possession, while the second indicates that the thing possessed is immediately with the possessor, perhaps in his hand or on his person. It is also used to indicate more intimate possession, even if the thing possessed is not on one's person. Examples include **si mange love** "there-is me-to money," *i.e.* "I have money," **love si amenge** "money there-is us-to," *i.e.* "we have money," **si le rakleske love** "there-is the boy-to money," *i.e.* "the boy has money."

d) Another way of forming a possessive construction is by means of the preposition **ka** followed by the noun or pronoun with or without {**-te**}: **ka leste si love** "to him-to is money", *i.e.* "he has money," **love ka tj'o phral naj** "there-is-not money to your brother," *i.e.* "your brother doesn't have money."

e) The general negative "have not" uses **naj** instead of **si**: **naj mande love** "I don't have money," **naj le rakleste love** "the boy doesn't have money. Compare these with **ma naj mange love** "I have no money," **ma naj le rakleske love** "the boy has no money."

f) A slightly different, and far less common, negative possessive construction uses **či** followed by the possessive pronoun plus the noun, thus **či leski Rromni** "he doesn't have a wife," **či lako mobìli** "she doesn't have a car" (compare these with **nìči leski Rromni** "not his wife," **naj lako mobìli** "it isn't her car").

g) Expressions of possession are so common, that the full form of the pronoun, with its postposition, is frequently not employed. Instead, just the short form, minus any suffix, is used: **naj ma love** (for **naj mande love**) "I don't have money," **naj tu love**, &c. In fact the equivalent of the *HAVE* verb, with its pronouns, could be represented thus:

si ma	"I have"	**naj ma**	"I don't have"
si tu	"you have"	**naj tu**	"you don't have"
si les	"he has"	**naj les**	"he doesn't have"
si la	"she has"	**naj la**	"she doesn't have"
si ame	"we have"	**naj ame**	"we don't have"
si tume	"you have"	**naj tume**	"you don't have"
si le(n)	"they have"	**naj le(n)**	"they don't have"

These short forms may be used with the corresponding pronouns to their right or left, thus **o raklo, si les love** "the boy, there-is him(-to) money," *i.e.* "the boy has money," **naj len kak love, murre phral** "my brothers don't have any money."

h) The equivalents of the future tense and the conditional mood of *BE* are expressed with forms of √**av-** "(be)come," which are discussed more fully on page 103 below. For the purpose of providing the complete paradigm for the possessive verbal forms, however, they are included here:

si les	"he has"
sas les	"he had"
avela les	"he will have"
te avela les	"that he'll have" (**t'al les**)
te avilino les	"if he'd had" (**t'av'lino les**)

naj les	"he hasn't"
nas les	"he hadn't"
či avela les	"he won't have"
te na avela les	"that he won't have" (**te n'a'l les**)
te na avèlas les	"if he hadn't" (**te n'à'las les**)
te na avilino les	"if he hadn't had" (**te n'av'lino les**)

Les alternates with **leste** or **leske** throughout.

Remember that if what is possessed is plural, the verb √**av-** must also be plural. Nouns such as **love** "money," **bal** "hair," **zeja** "back, spine" are plural, not singular nouns, so you would say

avena les love	"he will have money"
te avena les love	"that he'll have money"
te avena les lundži bal	"if he had long hair"
te aviline les zorale zeja	"if he'd had a strong back"

These last two constructions are more commonly heard as **te sas les lundži bal** and **te sas les zorale zeja**.

Verbs: Those Followed by Dative Pronouns

A number of verbs in Romani are constructed in much the same way as in colloquial English "we ate us a ham," "I drank me a beer," employing the dative personal pronouns. Examples are:

xasa amenge ekh balo	"we'll eat a pig"
pen tumenge bìrja	"you're drinking beer"
dža te soves tuke	"go and sleep"
phirdem mange	"I went for a walk"

Verbs: Past Tenses: The Aorist

The *aorist* tense in Romani is used to express various past actions, and partly overlaps with the English preterite in function. It would be the tense used in all of these sentences: "I saw the house," "I sang each week at the club," "I've already eaten it" and "I've been to the movies six times already this week." These are not all preterite constructions in English.

The aorist is based upon an aorist stem, which consists of the root plus an NFA, plus a suffix to indicate person and number and sometimes gender. This root is usually, though not always, the same as the present tense root; aorists can therefore be divided into regular and irregular categories. The frame for regularly constructed aorists is

AORIST ROOT + *NFA* + PERSON/NUMBER SUFFIX

The NFA is either an {-*l*-} or a {-*d*-}, depending upon what consonant occurs before it; if the aorist root ends in any of the alveo-dental series [n], [l], [d] or [r], the NFA will be {-*d*-}, although /-d/ plus {-*d*-} will be written singly, as <-d->. If the root ends in any other consonant, then the NFA will be {-*l*-}, although /-l/ plus {-*l*-} is written singly, as <-l->. The combination of the aorist root and the aorist NFA is called the aorist stem. If the root ends in a /-v/, both NFAs are possible, although this /-v/ will disappear before it (*cf.* √amblav- and √anzuv-, below).

Regular Aorist Roots

These are regular because they have the same aorist root as the present tense root; some of them behave irregularly in other ways, and are discussed separately. Those occurring with the NFA {-*d*-} include the following. Those verbs which take objects are indicated by *tr.* where this is not clear:

adžuker-	"wait (for)," "expect"
akhar-	"call"
an-	"bring"
ambla(v)-	"hang" *tr.*

ambòld-	"turn," "return," "revolve"
anger-	"carry," "lead," "direct"
ankala(v)-	"pull out," "extract," "extend" *tr.*
anker-	"hold," "contain," "keep"
anzar-	"pass (to)," "hand (to)"
athar-	"cheat"
ara(v)-	"dismantle," "pull down"
baga(v)-	"sing"
biča(v)-	"send"
bikin-	"sell"
bister-	"forget"
bol-	"dip"
čala(v)-	"hit," "whip," "strike"
čičid-	"squeeze"
cìrd-	"pull," "move," "suck" *tr.*
čhin-	"cut"
čhor-	"pour"
čhùd-	"throw"
čor-	"steal"
čumìd-	"kiss"
d-	"give"
dandar-	"bite"
dara-	"fear"
duna(v)-	"roll up," "fold up" *tr.*
džin-	"count," "read"
gara(v)-	"hide," "guard," "keep" *tr.*
haljer-	"understand"
hula(v)-	"share," "separate," "comb"
huna(v)-	"dig"
hurja(v)-	"dress" *tr.*
ker-	"do," "make," "owe," "cost"
khu(v)-	"weave," "braid"
kìd-	"pack," "collect," "gather"
kira(v)-	"cook"
kurr-	"copulate"
lada(v)-	"load up," "pack"
ličar-	"mash," "crush"
mar-	"hit"

mor-	"polish," "scrub"
mudar-	"kill"
murra(v)-	"shave," "scrape"
najar-	"swim"
parikẹr-	"thank"
phard-	"threaten"
phen-	"say," "tell"
phẹr-	"fill up" *tr.*
phir-	"walk"
phụtjar-	"swell up," "expand"
phùrd-	"blow," "breathe"
pokin-	"pay"
porra(v)-	"stretch," "widen"
pravar-	"feed" *tr.*
prịndžẹr-	"recognise," "know"
pụtẹr-	"open," "undo," "untie"
ròd-	"seek," "look for"
sẹr-	"remember"
sikha(v)-	"show," "demonstrate"
sikjar-	"teach," "train"
su(v)-	"sew"
šar-	"praise"
tasa(v)-	"strangle," "drown" *tr.*
tẹrdjar-	"stop" *tr.*
tràd-	"send," "travel," "drive"
tho-	"put," "place"
vàzd-	"pick up"
xala(v)-	"wash"
xanrrùnd-	"scratch"
xasar-	"lose"
xutil-	"catch," "grab"

Those with the aorist NFA {-*l*-} include the following:

akuš-	"scold," "insult"
anzu(v)-	"reach for, extend"
arakh-	"find," "guard"
arẹs-	"arrive," "reach"

baš-	"make a noise," "play an instrument," "bark," "growl"
beš-	"sit," "stay," "reside"
čamb-	"chew"
čarr-	"lick"
dikh-	"look," "see"
duš-	"milk"
kam-	"desire," "want"
khap-	"drink liquor"
khel-	"dance," "play"
khos-	"wipe," "polish"
l-	"take"
makh-	"wipe," "smear"
mang-	"want," "beg"
mukh-	"let," "allow," "leave"
nakh-	"pass," "cross over," "happen"
naš-	"flee", "elope"
phag-	"break" *tr.*
pharru(v)-	"die"
pi-	"drink," "smoke"
piš-	"grind"
pučh-	"ask"
puš-	"stab," "pierce"
ta(v)-	"cook"
xa-	"eat"

Aorist Person and Number Suffixes

Using √**phir-** "walk" as an example, the following are the aorist tense person and number endings:

me	phir-d-em	"I walked"	-em
tu	phir-d-(j)an	"you walked"	-(j)an
vov	phir-d-(j)a(s)	"he walked"	-(j)a(s)
voj	phir-d-(j)a(s)	"she walked"	-(j)a(s)
ame	phir-d-(j)am	"we walked"	-(j)am
tume	phir-d-(j)an	"you walked"	-(j)an
von	phir-d-(in)e	"they walked"	-(in)e

Some Vlax dialects, *e.g.* Eastern Kalderash, have a [j]-sound in the terminations; others, *e.g.* Lovaritska, don't have this feature (Kalderash **phirdjan**, Lovari **phirdan**).

Most dialects of Romani have the suffix {-(j)om} in the first person singular, rather than {-em}: **me dikhljom** "I saw." In contact areas, this has been acquired by Vlax speakers as well.

The third person singular ending {-(j)as-} is usually {-ja} in ordinary speech, but is {-jas} in careful speech, or if the pluperfect ending {-as} (page 98) is joined to it (**phirdjàsas** "he had walked").

The third person plural ending is usually {-e}, but this varies with {-ine}. Sometimes it is a matter of established preference, *e.g.* **von dikhle** ~ **von dikhline** "they saw;" sometimes it is because the aorist stem is very short, thus **line, dine** (instead of *le, *de "they took," "they gave" — and in some dialects even **linem, dinem, dikhlinem**, &c.), while in other dialects, it expresses a different verbal mood, the past conditional (see page 97): **dikhle** "they saw," **dikhline** "they would have seen."

Irregular Aorist Forms

A number of common verbs have irregular aorist forms, which must be learnt individually. They are listed here in the third person singular to indicate that some of them, including a substantial number of thematic verbs, keep {-a-} in the present tense verb endings throughout (**darav, daras, daral, daras, daran, daran**). note also that some verbs are inflected for gender in the aorist third person singular (**anklisto, anklisti**). Also included here are some which have irregular third person present tense forms.

3rd Sg. Present		3rd Sg. Aorist		Aorist Stem
ačhel	"he waits"	**ačhilo**	"he waited"	**ačhil-**
anklel	"he mounts"	**anklisto**	"he mounted"	**anklist-**
asal	"he laughs"	**asaja**	"he laughed"	**asa-**
avel	"he comes"	**avilo**	"he came"	**avil-**
bilal	"it thaws"	**biljajlo**	"it thawed"	**biljajl-**

bučhuv-	"he is named"	bučhlja	"he was named"	bučh-
čhadel-pe[1]	"he vomits"	čhaglo-pe	"he vomited"	čhagl-
džal	"he goes"	gelo	"he went"	gel-
džanel	"he knows"	džanglja	"he knew"	džangl-
gilàbal	"he sings"	gilabadja	"he sang"	gilabad-
hulel	"he descends"	hulisto	"he descended"	hulist-
hurjal	"he flies"	hurjajlo	"he flew"	hurjajl-
istral	"he skids"	istrajlo	"he skidded"	istrajl-
izdral	"he trembles"	izdrajlo	"he trembled"	izdrajl-
kàndel	"he obeys"	kanglja	"he obeyed"	kangl-
katal	"he spins"	kaklja	"he spun"	kakl-
khàndel	"he stinks"	khanglja	"he stank"	khangl-
lošal	"he smiles"	lošaja	"he smiled"	loša-
merel	"he dies"	mulo	"he died"	mul-
mol	"it costs"	modja	"it cost"	mod-
mothol	"he says"	mothodja	"he said"	mothod-
patjal	"he believes"	patjaja	"he believed"	patja-
perel	"he falls"	pelo	"he fell"	pel-
pitjal	"it drips"	pitjaja	"it dripped"	pitja-
prasal	"he mocks"	prasaja	"he mocked"	prasa-
pràstel	"he runs"	prastaja	"he ran"	prasta-
phàndel	"he shuts"	phanglja	"he shut"	phangl-
rovel	"he weeps"	ruja	"he wept"	ru-
rràndel	"he scratches"	rranglja	"he scratched"	rrangl-
rrondjal	"it thunders"	rrondjaja	"it thundered"	rrondja-
sovel	"he sleeps"	suto	"he slept"	sut-
sungal	"he smells"	sungaja	"he smelt"	sunga-
tasuvel	"he drowns"	tasulo	"he drowned"	tasul-
thol	"he puts"	thodja	"he put"	thod-
tromal	"he dares"	tromajlo	"he dared"	tromajl-
uštel	"he arises"	uštilo	"he arose"	uštil-
xandjol	"he itches"	xandjulo	"he itched"	xandjul-
xasal	"he laughs"	xasaja	"he laughed"	xasa-
xasàvel	"he vanished"	xasajlo	"he vanished"	xasajl-
xlel-pe[1]	"he defecates"	xindja-pe	"he defecated"	xind-
xutjel	"he jumps"	xuklo	"he jumped"	xukl-

[1]This is a reflexive verb, discussed on page 140. The reflexive pronoun is hyphenated.

94

More on Imperatives

A number of the verbs in the above lists have non-final stress. These include **ambòldel, cìrdel, čumìdel, čhàdel-pe, čhùdel, gilàbal, kàndel, khàndel, kìdel, phàndel, phùrdel, pràstel, ròdel, rràndel, tràdel, xanrrùndel, xasàvel** and **vàzdel**. It is clear that for some of these at least, they are historically noun plus verb (√d- "give") combinations, *e.g.* **kàndel** "obey" = **kan del**, "ear he-gives"[1]. The singular imperative for these is made by keeping the non-final stress and adding {-e} to the stem: **čumìde, čhùde, kànde,** &c.[2] The plural imperative adds an {-n} to this: **čumìden,** &c.

Verbs which maintain the /-a-/ vowel throughout in the present tense suffixes (here, they are **asal, bašal, bilal, daral, gilàbal, hurjal, istral, izdral, katal, lošal, patjal, pitjal, prasal, rrondjal, sungal, tromal** and **xasal**), keep this in the singular imperative, and take {-an} in the plural: **hurja! baša!, na troman! na xasan!.**

Verbs with an /-i-/, which is realized as a /-j-/ in the first person present tense ending, *e.g.* **ankljav** but **anklel** (here they are **ankljav, huljav, uštjav, xlja(v)-ma** and **xutjav**) keep this in the imperative: **ankli!, huli!, ušti!, xli-tu!,** &c. The /-i-/ is not maintained in the plural imperative: **anklen!, hulen!, ušten!.** A mnority of speakers carry the /-i-/ throughout for all persons: **ankljav, ankljes, ankljel.**

Athematic verbs take {-sar} in the imperative in both the singular and the plural. These are dealt with on page 117.

Imperative particles

The word **nàdal** can be used as an emphatic negative imperative marker, though its use is considered abrupt and it is best avoided: **nàdal beš tele!** "don't sit down!," **nàdal cìrden!** "don't (pl.) move!."

The particles **ba** and **ta** can also be added to imperatives to

---

[1]Cf. also √**motho-** "speak," < **mo-**, oblique root of **muj** "mouth," plus √**tho-** "put."
[2]In the case of nominal compound nouns, it would be more accurate to state this as adding **de** (imperative of "give") to the root.

give them extra force: **šun-ba**! "listen!," **beš-ta**! "sit," **àke-ta** "here it is!.." As emphatic tags, they are hyphenated in print. By themselves, these words mean "certainly:" **ba či**! "certainly not!," **ba ke nìči**!, "not at all!," **ta tu či mjazos zdràveno** "you certainly don't look well!," **ba me či džav** "I'm certainly not going." *Cf.* also **phureja ba xaraneja**! "oh wise old man!.."

Verbs: The Present Participle

This is formed from the present tense root, to which is added the suffix {-(i)-ndoj}: √dža- "go," **džajndoj** "going," √rov- "weep," **rovindoj** (pronounced [rojndoj]) "weeping;" **maladjilem la rovindoj** "I met her weeping" (*i.e.* her weeping, not me); **dem pe lende sa džinindoj** "I found them all reading," *or* "I found them doing nothing but reading."

The present participle is much more common in non-Vlax Romani dialects, where it has various related forms (*e.g.* {-i-ndos} or {-i-ndor} in Serbia and Albania). In Vlax, its equivalent is more often constructed with the present indicative and **te**: **dem pe lende te džinènas** "I encountered them all reading," **ašunàvas les te gilàbal** "I was listening to him sing(ing)," **me šundem les te dèlas dùma francuzìcka** "I heard him speaking French" (*cf.* **me šundem ke dèlas dùma francuzìcka** "I heard that he was speaking French.")

One instance of this verbal suffix being added to a noun is the word **phirasandoj** "joking," from the feminine noun **phiras** "a joke; fun."

Verbs: The Past Participle

The past participle of a verb functions as an adjective. It consists of the aorist stem plus the appropriate adjectival endings (page 74). Thus the aorist stem **čhind-** of the verb √**čhin-** "cut" is also its past participle stem:

o gadžo čhinel o šelo	"the man cuts the string"	čhin-
o gadžo čhindja o šelo	"the man cut the string"	čhin-d-
o šelo naj čhindo	"the string isn't cut"	čhin-d-*o*

e krjànga naj čhindi	"the branch isn't cut"	čhin-d-*i*
la čhinda krjangasa	"with the cut branch"	čhin-d-*a*
le čhinde krjanganca	"with the cut branches"	čhin-d-*e*

Some third person aorists already have the same form as the past participle. These are the aorists of verbs which are already marked for gender, such as **čhaglo, xuklo, kanglo, khanglo, phanglo, rranglo** and so on (see pages 88*ff.*). These may sometimes result in ambiguous constructions, thus **o Rrom našlo** could mean either "the man fled" or "the runaway man." This can be avoided either by using other verbal forms, *e.g.* causatives (pages 127*ff.*), or by incorporating a rule into the standardized grammar which would syntactically restrict past participles to the pre-nominal position. *Cf.* also the disambiguated construction **o Rrom o našlo** (discussed on page 115).

The verbs √**l**- "take" and √**d**- "give" have the past participial stems **lin-** and **din-** respectively.

Some verbs which have aorist stems which correspond in the third person with their past participial stems also have regularly-formed aorists, but for speakers who make such a distinction, a semantic difference exists. In the case of the verb √**mer-** "die," for instance, the past participle stem is **mul-** "dead," which is also the aorist stem:

e luludji merel	"the flower is dying"
e luludji muli	"the flower died"
e muli luludji	"the dead flower"

The regularly-derived aorist stem **merd-** would be used if the event was not an immediate one. **E luludji muli** would mean that the flower had suddenly, or very recently, died, while **e luludji merdja** would mean that it had occurred at some earlier time (*cf.* also **mulano** or **murdalo**, which are used *only* as adjectives). Other verbs which have two third person aorist forms, and for which the same semantic differentiation applies, include **avilo ~ avilja** "came," and **bešlo ~ bešlja** "sat."

Athematic verbs form their past participles differently, and these are discussed on page 119.

Verbs: The Past Conditional Mood

Some dialects of Vlax Romani have a past conditional mood which is formed by inserting the NFA {-in-} before the person-number ending of the aorist stem:

čhin-el	"he cuts"
čhin-d-ja	"he cut"
čhin-d-o(-i/-a/-e)	"cut," past participle
čhin-d-in-o	"he would have cut"
čhin-d-in-i	"she would have cut"
čhin-d-in-e	"they would have cut"
ker-el	"he does"
ker-d-ja	"he did"
ker-d-o(-i/-a/-e)	"done," past participle
ker-d-in-o	"he would have done"
ker-d-in-i	"she would have done"
ker-d-in-e	"they would have done"

te andindjam amare love, potjindindjam lake dades
"if we had brought our money, we would have paid her father"
akhardindem tut te džanglem ke sanas khere
"I would have called you if I'd known you were home"
avile aratji   "they came yesterday"
aviline aratji "they would have come yesterday"

For Vlax speakers in America who descended from the first migration, this distinction appears not to have been maintained; the {-in-} NAF has lost its grammatical function, and occurs only as a variant form of the third person plural aorist: **bešle ~ bešline** "they stayed, they sat." it is not heard in the singular. It may be the case that the grammatical distinction is a development which has taken place in European Vlax since the first migrations to North America in the late 19th Century.

In American Kalderash, the past conditional is constructed with **te** (**te àla** in Machvano Vlax) "if," plus the pluperfect tense, discussed next:

gelem lasa thaj arakhlja o than
"I went with her and she found the place."
te gelèmas lasa, arakhljàsas o than
"if I'd gone with her, she would have found the place."

Alternatively, the suffix {**-as**} may be joined to the future marker **kam** (discussed on the next page).

Verbs: The Pluperfect Tense

If an action was already completed at some time referred to in the past, this is expressed in Vlax by adding the unstressed suffix {**-as**} to the full form of the aorist (compare this use of the same suffix with the present tense to form the imperfect, on page 84):

dikh-àv	"I see"	*Present*
dikh-àv-as	"I was seeing, used to see"	*Imperfect*
dikh-l-èm	"I saw"	*Aorist*
dikh-l-èm-as	"I had seen"	*Pluperfect*

The third person aorist singular must be in its full /-s/ form, (*i.e.* **dikhljas** and not ***dikhlja**), and irregular third persons which are gender-marked (**bešlo, bešli**) must be put into the regular paradigm (**bešljas**):

dikhljàsas	"s/he had seen"
rujàsas	"s/he had wept"
geljàsas	"s/he had gone"
aviljàsas	"s/he had come"
bešljàsas	"s/he had stayed"
xasajljàsas	"s/he had disappeared"

The third person plural aorist must also take an /-s/ before affixing the perfective {**-as**}:

dikhlèsas	"they had seen"
mukhlèsas	"they had left"
avilèsas	"they had come"

Verbs: The Future Tense

There are three ways of forming the future tense, not counting the use of the present tense which can also be used in future constructions. The first is by adding {-a} to the present finite stem, with no shift of stress:

dikh-àv	"I see"	**dikh-às**	"we see"
dikh-àv-a	"I shall see"	**dikh-às-a**	"we shall see"
dikh-ès	"you see"	**dikh-èn**	"you see"
dikh-ès-a	"you will see"	**dikh-èn-a**	"you will see"
dikh-èl	"s/he sees"	**dikh-èn**	"they see"
dikh-èl-a	"s/he will see"	**dikh-èn-a**	"they will see"

This is also the *oratorical* form of the present tense, which is used in speeches, dignified address and so on (discussed further on page 142).

These constructions with {-a} cannot occur after **te** when that particle links two successive verbs to express the equivalent of the English infinitive (see page 78):

veṣẹlova-ma te dikhav tut   "I shall be happy to see you"
zumavasa te žutis len   "we shall try to help them"
phụterena o vudar lenge   "they'll open the door for them"

A second future construction, called the analytical future, places the word **kam** before the present tense verb form. Some writers join it to the following verb with a hyphen. This is a calque on constructions found in some Balkan languages, and probably has its origin in Byzantine Greek: **kam dikhav** "I shall see," **kam dikhes** "you'll see."

This is pronounced [kan] before dentals, and [ka] in rapid speech; in some Vlax dialects spoken in the southern Balkans, it has the form **kame**. Note too that in some kinds of Vlax, specifically varieties of Polish Lovaritska, **kam** has the meaning "maybe." Because of this, constructions of the above type do not exist, the future being constructed only with suffixed {-a}. The potential for

100

ambiguity can result in *e.g.* Kalderash **kam kerel les** "he will do it" being interpreted as "maybe he'll do it."

There is another construction in at least one variety of Vlax which might be called the intentional future, and which uses √**dža-** "go" plus the verb, without a linking *te*: **vov džal bikinel p'o mobìli** "he's going to sell his car." This construction is heard in the Kalderash spoken in France, and is found in the translations of the gospels produced in that country. It is probably a calque on French, e.g. *il va vendre son auto*; it is not heard in American Vlax. The future marker **va** (< Romanian *a voi* "want," 3rd pers. sg.) with the {-a} future is found in Romanian Vlax: **me va džava** "I'll go."

Verbs: The Future Perfect

In combination with the aorist, the future particle **kam** gives the future perfect: **me kam dikhlem les**, "I shall have seen him," **kam kerdjan tj'i butji**, "you will have done your work."

Verbs: The Present Conditional

Kam can also take the affix {-as} (*pp.* 84 and 98) to express the present conditional mood when used before the present tense:
kàmas dikhav   "I would see"
kàmas kerav les te pučhes mandar "I would do it if you asked me"
The past conditional mood, discussed on page 97, took the suffix {-as} on the aorist (**dikhlèm***as* "I would have seen"). An alternative form of the past conditional places this suffix on **kam** and not on the aorist: **kàm***as* **dikhlem** "I would have seen."

Verbs: The Suffix {*-tar*}

There exists in Romani a non-stressed suffix {-tar} which may be added to verbs of direction or motion, such as √**dža-** "go," √**pràst-** "run," √**naš-** "flee," √**lang-** "limp," √**av-** "come," &c., to express the notion of "off" or "away." It is a different morpheme from postpositional {-tar}. This can move very freely within the verbal cluster:

te teljaràs*tar* akana!	"let's set off now!"
našèlas*tar* lestar	"she was running away from him"
tradjam*tar* dur	"we travelled far away"
k'ekh aver them geljàsas*tar*	"he'd gone away to another country"
džastar ka*tar*	"let's be going from here"
hàj*tar*	"come here" (*see* hàjde, next page).

Verbs: Other Special Verbs and Verbal Modifiers

Besides **kam** and **kàmas**, there are a number of other verbs and adverbal modifiers which do not conform to the regular pattern. These include the following:

a) **Mol** "it is worth," has no other forms in most varieties of Vlax, although speakers of some dialects have retained **mov** "I am worth," **mos** "you are worth," &c. **Sòde mol?** "what is it worth?," "how much does it cost?".

b) The verb √**àl-** "see here" survives only in the imperative in American Vlax: **àle!** "here, take this!," **àlen** "here you (pl.) are!". In Romanian Vlax it is still a productive verb: **àlav, àles** (*NB* the third person singular aorist masculine and feminine **alo, ali**).

c) **Phènke** "he says," "she says," "they say" (or *said*) is invariable, having no other forms. It is used where appropriate as a pause-filler in narrated direct speech: "**no, phènke, so gindis?**" "Well, he says, what d'you think?".

d) **Vaštenkuj** means "pretend to," and is placed directly before the verb: **vaštenkuj geli and'o kher** "she pretended to go into the house."

e) **Sa** (or **sja** for some speakers) has as its primary meaning "all," but placed before verbs it can mean both "still" and "doing nothing but:" **sa kiravèlas kàna avilem khere** "she was still cooking when I came home," **so sas von te keren lengi butji, sa khelènas** "instead of doing their work, they were doing nothing but play."

f) **Sòma** or **d'àba** before a verb means "(only) just:" **sòma dikhlem les** "I only just saw him," **d'àba aresli** "she's just arrived."

g) **Šaj** means "can," "be able," **me šaj šoljaziv** "I can whistle." This word has no other form, but the verb √**dast-** "be able" is fully declinable: **dastil te šoljazil** "she can whistle." Some speakers follow **šaj** by **te: šaj te šoljazil.**

h) **Našti** means "cannot," "not be able:" **me našti šoljaziv** "I cannot whistle." This word has no other form, but the verb √**našt-** "not be able" is fully declinable: **naštil te šoljazil** "she can't whistle." The athematic form of this verb (and of √**dast-**) suggests that they are innovations in the language. Some speakers follow **našti** by **te: našti te šoljazil.**

i) **Mùsaj** means "must." This is followed by the appropriate dative noun or pronoun plus **te: mùsaj mange te ačhav** "I must remain," **mùsaj tuke te džas** "you must go," **mùsaj le rakleske te terdjol** "the boy must stop." Very frequently, however, the inflected pronoun, and even the **te**, is omitted, thus **mùsaj te ačhav** or **mùsaj ačhav**, forms which should be avoided in formal speech. Note also *mus'* **te ačhav.** The past is constructed with **sas** either before or after **mùsaj: sas mùsaj leske te xal** or **mùsaj sas leske te xal** "he had to eat." **Mùsaj** is negated with **na** (**nas** in the past) and not **či: na mùsaj lenge te keren les** "they mustn't do it."

j) **Hàjde** or sometimes **hàjdi** means both "let's go" and "come here" or "come on." Although it is probably of Romanian origin, it has been reanalysed in Romani as if it were **haj + de**, where **de** is interpreted as a shortening of **(v)orde, (v)arde** "here." *Cf.* the form **hàjtar**, and the similar **adarde**, which mean the same as **hàjde.**

k) The single verb **fal** (or **faj** in Hungarian Lovaritska[1]) followed by an oblique case noun or pronoun means "it seems:" **fal ma ke či amboldena** "it seems to me that they won't come back." This has the past tense **fajlja** or **fàlas: fajlja la čhake ke vuže sas khere lako dad** "it seemed to the girl that her father was already home," **fàlas murra phenjake ke xoli sas mange** "it seemed to my sister that I was angry." Another way of saying "it seems" or "it appears" is with the verb **dikh-jo-** "be seen" (page 125): **dikhlili ke kašuki sas** "she gave the appearance of being deaf."

l) There is a fully conjugated verb √**trub-u-** (for some speakers √**trob-u-**) "need to," but other personal forms are not used

---

[1]Because of interference from Hungarian phonology, /l/ disappears in the environment of some vowels, thus Hungarian Lovaritska *faj*, *volij*, *kaji* for what in other Vlax dialects are **fal** "it seems," **volil** "he loves," **kali** "black," &c.

so often as its third person singular, both present, **trubul** (**trubuj** in Hungarian Lovaritska), and past, **trubùlas**[1]. This is followed by the dative noun or pronoun, which may optionally be omitted, plus **te**: **trubul te parruvav 'e càlja** "I need to change my clothes," **trubùlas leske maj kašt** "he needed more wood."

Verbs: *BE*: Expressing the Future

The future of *BE* is expressed with the verb √**av**- "(be)come," forming what is sometimes called the ingressive copula construction:

baro si	"he's big"	**baro avel**	"he will be big"
baro lo	"he's big"	**baro avel**	"he will be big"
bare le	"they're big"	**baro aven**	"they will be big"

Some speakers put √**av**- into the future tense for this construction:

baro avela or **kam avel baro**   "he'll be big"

Remember to use the correct third person plural form of this verb in future possessive constructions (page 87):

avena ma duj mobìlja "I'll have two cars."

All Forms of *BE*

All forms of *BE* are given here in the third person singular and plural:

vov si	"he is"	**von si**	"they are"
vov sas	"he was"	**von sas**	"they were"
vov avela	"he will be"	**von avena**	"they will be"
vov kam avel	"he will be"	**von kam aven**	"they will be"
te vov avel	"that he be"	**te von aven**	"that they be"
te vov av(è)las	"if he were"	**te von av(è)nas**	"if they were"
te vov av(i)lino	"if he'd been"	**te von av(i)line**	"if they'd been"

[1] This is the only {-u-} verb in Romani (**trubuv, trubus,** &c.), and has no doubt been created by analogy with other verbs. Its origin is in Romanian *trebui* "ought to."

Verbs: Expressing Obligation with *BE*

Although obligation can be expressed using the indeclinable athematic **mùsaj** (page 102), there is a thematic construction with the *BE* verb which may also be used. English can also do this: "you *are* to stay here," "I *am* to report back," "he *was* to marry her."

Romani constructs these in the same way: **tu** *san* **te ačhes katka, me** *sim* **te pirriv pàlpale, vov** *sas* **te ansuril lasa** (besides the "must" forms **mùsaj (tuke) te ačhes katka, mùsaj (mange) te pirriv pàlpale, mùsaj (leske) te ansuril lasa.**

Like English also, Romani can express obligation with *HAVE*, as in "I *have* to go," "he *has* to marry her," &c., thus *si* **mande te džav,** *si* **leste te ansuril lasa,** &c.

Adverbs

Adverbs fall into two broad categories, regular and irregular. Regular adverbs may be derived from adjectives, prepositions, other adverbs or nouns. In Romani, the regular adverbial adjectival suffix is {**-es**}, which is affixed to the root, just as is done in English by adding {*-ly*}: "happy" → "happi*ly*."

√**bar-**	"big"	√**bidjind-**	"uncounted"
bares	"largely"	**bidjindes**	"countlessly"
√**šukar**	"beautiful"	√**tang**	"narrow"
šukares	"beautifully"	**tanges**	"narrowly"
√**phar-**	"heavy"	√**Rroman-**	"Gypsy"
phares	"heavily"	**Rromanes**	"in the Gypsy way"
√**ivand**	"raw"	√**gadžikan-**	"non-Gypsy"
ivandes	"rudely"	**gadžikanes**	"in the non-Gypsy way"

The adverbial forms for nationalities or groups, *e.g. Rromanes* are used when referring to language, dress, behavior, &c., thus **šaj vrakeres Rromanes?** "can you speak Romani (*i.e.* "Gypsily")?, **e Gèža hurjadjas-pe Rromanes** "Geža dresses Romani-fashion,"

kiradem e zumi Rromanes "I cooked the soup in the Romani way."

Adverbs from Prepositions

a) Adverbs are regularly derived from certain prepositions (page 73), as well as from other adverbs, by the addition of the suffix {-al}:

andre	"inside"	**andral**		"internally, within"
àngla	"in front of"	**anglal**		"in front"
krugom	"around"	**krujal (trujal)**		"roundabout"
maškar	"among, between"	**maškaral**		"in the middle"
opre	"up"	**opral**		"above"
pàla	"behind"	**palal**		"at the back"
pàša	"near"	**pašal**		"nearby, adjoining"
tèla	"under"	**telal**		"underneath"

Note also

intja	"that way"	**intjal**	"across"
(v)orde	"here"	**(v)ordal**	"at this place"

b) The suffix {-al} may also derive adverbs from a number of nouns and adjectives:

agor	"end, edge"	**agoral**	"at the end, edge"
čor	"thief"	**čorjal**	"stealthily, in secret"
drom	"road"	**dromal**	"by road, on the road"
kher	"house"	**kheral**	"from home"
kothe	"there"	**kothal**	"therefore, thereupon"
kotor	"piece, part"	**kotoral**	"partly"
muj	"face"	**mujal**	"upside down"
rig	"side, edge"	**rigal**	"at the side, on the edge"
šero	"head"	**šeral**	"at/from the top; mainly"
vast	"hand"	**vastal**	"by hand, in the hand"

Note also

dur	"far"	**dural**	"from afar"
stìngo	"left"	**stingal**	"on the left"

c) There is another set of adverbs sharing some of these same prepositional roots but which, like ***andre*** and ***opre*** end in {-e}:

angle	"forward, ahead"	(< àngla)
maškare	"in the middle"	(< maškar)
pàle	"once more"	(< pàla)
pàlpale	"back again, back(wards)"	(<pàla, with reduplication)
paše	"nearby"	(< pàša). *NB* not *pàše.
tele	"down(wards), below"	(<tèla). *NB* not *tèle.

d) Possibly related to this suffix is the now no longer productive nominal case ending {-e} (pronounced as stressed [ə́] in eastern Kalderash), which survives in a number of derived adverbials: These are:

bul	"buttocks"	*in* √d- bule	"copulate"
činisàra	"eve before a holiday"	činisare	"on a holiday eve"
djes	"day"	djese	"daily"
ivend	"winter"	ivende	"during winter"
Kričùno	"Christmas"	Kričune	"at Christmas"
kurko	"week; Sunday"	kurke	"on Sundays; weekly"
kher	"house"	khere	"to home, at home"
milaj[1]	"summer"	milaje	"during summer"
mindž	"vulva"	*in* √d- mindže	"copulate"
mizmèri	"noon"	mizmere	"at noon"
mjazùco	"noon"	mjazuce	"at noon"
primovàra	"springtime"	primovare	"during springtime"
rjat	"night"	rjate[2]	"at night; nightly"
Rrusàlja	"Whitsuntide"	Rrusalje	"at Whitsun"
tàmna	"autumn"	tamne	"during autumn"
žùno	"Christmas Eve"	žune	"on Christmas Eve"

e) A similar suffix with the same function is stressed {-ine}:

Patradji	"Easter"	Patradjine	"at Eastertime"
Lùja	"Monday"	Lujine	"on Monday(s)"
Màrci	"Tuesday"	Marcine	"on Tuesday(s)"
Tetradji	"Wednesday"	Tetradjine	"on Wednesday(s)"
Žòja	"Thursday"	Žojine	"on Thursday(s)"
Paraštuji	"Friday"	Paraštujine	"on Friday(s)"

---

[1]Also nilaj, linaj
[2]Also rjati

107

Sàvato	"Saturday"	**Savatone**	"on Saturday(s)"
Kurko	"Sunday"	**Kurkone**	"on Sunday(s)"
			(also **kurke**)

f) A few noun-derived adverbs are formed with the prefix {a-}:

djes	"day"	**adjes**	"today"
ivend	"winter"	**ajivend**	"this winter"
milaj	"summer"	**amilaj**	"this summer"
rjat	"night"	**arjat**	"tonight"
rjat	"night"	**aratji**	"last night; yesterday"

g) Time adverbials having the sense of *from* or *since* can be constructed using the formula **dę** or **d'** + *ROOT* (or *STEM*) + {-àra}. This is rare in North American Vlax dialects.

àba	"already"	d'àba	"just"
adjes	"today"	d'adjesàra	"as of today"
akana	"now"	d'akanàra	"from now on"
aratji	"yesterday"	d'aratjàra	"since yesterday"
arjat	"tonight"	d'arjatàra	"from tonight onwards"
atòska	"then" (Mach.)	d'atoskàra	"from then on"
atùnči	"then" (Kald.)	d'atunčàra	"from then on"
ivend	"winter"	d'ivendàra	"since winter"
Kurko	"Sunday"	dę Kurkàra	"since Sunday"
milaj	"summer"	dę milajàra	"since summer"
mizmèri	"noon"	dę mizmeràra	"since noon; from noon onwards"
rjat	"night"	dę kuratjàra	"since the day before yesterday"
tehàra	"tomorrow"	dę teharàra	"as of tomorrow"
tehàra	"tomorrow"	dę teharin	"as of tomorrow'
tehàra	"tomorrow"	dę teharinàra	"as of tomorrow"
terno	"young"	dę ternàra	"since childhood"

h) Irregular adverbs are divided into those of manner (answering *how*), those of time (answering *when*) and those of place (answering *where*), and are either individual words, or combinations of words which must be learnt separately. Also included in the category of adverbials are adverbial phrases which have the formula

PREPOSITION + NOUN PHRASE, thus

> *Manner*: "with the small hammer," "in a hurry," "on his own."
> *Time*:   "in the morning," "after an hour," "by lunchtime."
> *Place*: "over the wall," "on the roof," "under the baby's bed."

i) There are some adverbs which are commonly heard in European Vlax, but which have not been retained in most (though not all) American varieties. These include **kazom** "how much, how many," **kabor** "how big," **odobor** "that many ~," **gadibor** "that much of a ~."

Adverbs: Manner

ambòri(m)	"maybe"
če fjàlo	"what kind of"
dàži, dàže	"even"
dàži či	"not even"
dèbja	"barely, hardly, scarcely"
dẹfjal	"in no way"
dẹ gràba	"promptly"
dẹsa	"too, overly"
dikhasa	"maybe"
gadja	"thus, so"
i, ji, vi	"also, too, additionally, likewise"
ivja, jivja	"in vain, without purpose;" "free;" nevertheless, notwithstanding"
intàjna	"without purpose"
katji	"so (many)"
kaditji, gadiki	"so (many)"
kajtji	"so (many)"
kam	"maybe" (see page 99); "approximately"
kesav- + {-tar}	"so, such, such a" (**kesavestar dilo lo**
paštji, pašči	"nearly" "he's so stupid")
pàte	"really," "unless"
pra, prja	"too, overly"
samuči	"barely, scarcely, hardly"

Sar (de)	"how" (see note below)
Sòde	"how much"
sodegòdi	"inasfar as, inasmuch as"
sòdja	"how many"
savestar	"what kind of"
tìstara	"thoroughly; immediately"
vòrta	"really"

"*How*" is expressed in Vlax by **sar** followed by the particle **dę** ([də], from Romanian). **De** is also used before the adjectives in the following constructions:

sar de baro?	"how big?"
trin màjli de lùngo	"three miles long"
pìnda jàrdi de buxlo	"fifty yards wide"
štar rrùndurja de vučo	"four storeys high"
či phendem khànči de nasul pa tute	"I said nothing bad about you"

Other functions of {de} are illustrated in the following sentences:

o sàstri skuntęjil, de tato ke (or **kaj**) **si**
"the iron is giving off sparks, so hot is it"

e Rromni asàlas, de vèsolo ke (or **kaj**) **sas**
"the woman was laughing, so happy was she"

murri bibi muli de phuri
"my aunt died of (old) age"

phirdja kadiki de dur, ke xasajli
"she walked so far, she got lost"

či mangav te pijav la, de tato ke (or **kaj**) **si**
"I don't want to drink it, because it is so hot"

našti te gindil jàsno, de mato ke (or **kaj**) **si**
"he can't think clearly, so drunk is he"

de but ke (or **kaj**) **akušèlas, me či manglem te šunav**
"he was swearing so much, I didn't want to listen"

de but ke (or **kaj**) **cipisardja našti šundem**
"he shouted so much, I couldn't hear"

NOTE that no complementizer "that" is necessary in the above (which alternates with **de but ke cipisardja ke našti šundem**).

When it is followed by an adjective or an adverb, "*So*" may also be translated with **kaditji (de)**: **e Rromni asàlas, ke kaditji vèsolo sas** "the woman was laughing, so happy was she," **kaditji de pharo sas** "it was so heavy," **tu san katji šukar!** "you're so beautiful!"

     Kaditji has the variant forms **gaditji, kadiki, gadiki, kajtji, katji,** &c. Before nouns, it means "so much/so many:" **kaditji glàti** "so many children."

     Another construction having the same meaning uses **kasav-** "such (a)," "this kind of (a)" with the ablative suffix {**-tar**}:

kasavestar dilo lo "he's so stupid"
kasavendar dile le "they're so stupid"

     "*Why*" is translated by **ànda soste** (*lit.* "from what?"), with the common variant **sostar,** pronounced **'star** in ordinary speech.

Adverbs: Time

àba	"already"
agore, agoreste	"finally"
akana	"now"
akanak	"now"
akanaš	"immediately, right away"
and'e vùrma	"finally"
atòska (Mach.)	"then"
atùnči (Kald.)	"then"
butìvar (or **bùtvar**)	"often"
či maj	"never"
dẹ	"since"
dẹkin	"since"
dẹ sar	"since"
domult	"since long ago"
dži	"until, as far as"
dži ka	"as far as, up to"
dži pùn(e)	"until, as long as"
kàna	"when"
kàn'aj kàna	"occasionally"
maj anglal katar	"before" (see note below)
maj d'anglal	"first of all"

maj intuj	"first of all"
pànda	"still, yet"
pìnẹ, pùnẹ	"as long as, while, until"
pòšle, pòčhle	"later on" (usually with **maj**)
pùrmạ	"afterwards"
sòde	"how long" (**sòde džal tuke** "how long will it
stràzo	"soon" take you?")
šòha, šòxa	"never"
vàrvar	"sometimes"
vrjam(j)àsa	"eventually"
vunìvar	"sometimes"
vuže	"already"

Note the construction to translate both "before" and "after," *maj anglal katar (te)* and *maj palal katar (te)*:

maj anglal katar te džas andre, de ma tj'i bufàri
"before you go in, give me your wallet"
maj palal katar t'aves avri, dava la tuke pàlpale
"After you come out, I'll give it back to you"

Adverbs: Place

arde	"here"
athe	"here"
kaj	"where"
kajgòdi	"everywhere"
katar	"from where"
kathe	"here"
kathende	"nowhere; somewhere"
kathinende	"nowhere"
katka	"right here"
katkar	"from right here"
kothe	"there"
kothar	"from there"
kotka	"right there"
kotkar	"from right there"
kutka	"right over there"

kutkar	"from right over there"
odoring	"(in) that direction"
odoringar	"(in) that direction"
othe	"there"
(v)orde, (v)arde	"here"

Yes and *No*

In European Romani, "yes" is expressed by **àva**, and "no" by **na** or **nìč(i)**. In American Vlax, "yes" is usually **ej** or **je**; *ej* is also repeated during discourse by the listener to indicate that he is paying attention to what's being said. In both European and American Vlax, affirmation or negation is also expressed by **si** "(yes) it is" and **naj** "(no) it isn't." The verb itself may also be repeated thus:

avilo vuže khere?	"has he already come home?"
avilo	"(yes) he's come"
č'avilo	"(no) he hasn't come"

Conjunctions

Some of these in Romani are:

àle	"but" (see note below)
ànda kodja	"thereupon, and then"
àpo, àpoj	"thereupon, and then"
bàrem	"although, even though"
či...či	"neither...nor"
dàži ke	"even if"
dẹkin	"since, on account of, being that"
dẹ sar	"since, on account of, being that"
dži kaj	"until"
fînka	"since, on account of, because"
gadja...sar	"as...as"
ivja ke	"though"
jàkạ	"due to"

kadja kẹ	"in order that, in order to"
kàštẹ	"in order that, so that"
kẹ	"because"
màkar kẹ	"although"
màkar te	"even if"
načàjno	"nevertheless"
nitàla	"although, even though"
nùma, 'ma, nùmaj	"but, except that" (see note below)
pàrka	"as if, as though"
pàte	"unless"
p'òrmẹ, p'ùrmẹ	"and then, afterwards"
sajal	"however"
sa kadja	"so, therefore, in that case"
sar pàrka	"as though, as if"
so fèri	"except"
ta	"in order that, in order to" (see *p.* 113); "but"
te na	"unless"
thaj, haj, aj	"and"
thaj...thaj	"both...and"
vaj, vàjka	"or"
vèska, vìska	"because; as if, as though"
vi te	"even if, even though"
vor, vòrka	"or"

There are several words for *but* in the Romani dialects. In Europe, **àle, dja, dẹ** and **nùma** are found, though not as alternative forms in the same dialect. In some dialects, **nùma** or **nùmaj** is used to mean "only" and not "but" (*cf.* English "there were but three of them"). In American Vlax, **'ma, nùma** or **nùma kẹ** are most often heard, though the English word *but* is common for an increasing number of speakers.

Demonstratives

Demonstratives are the words for "this," "that," "these" and "those." They function as adjectives, and must agree in gender, number and case with the nouns they accompany. A distinction appears to be made, at least for some speakers, in the choice of demonstrative, depending upon whether the noun focus has already been introduced into the discourse or not, thus the demonstrative **kako** might be used with, *e.g.* **Rrom** the first time the word occurs, but **gado**, referring to the same noun, might be used thereafter.

Romani has very many demonstratives, which differ considerably from dialect to dialect. In Vlax, there is a "near - close - distant" relationship indicated in the vowels /a/ /o/ /u/ of the root (*cf.* **kathe** "here," **kothe** "there"). The most common demonstratives in Vlax are the following:

	This		*That*	
	Subject	*Oblique*	*Subject*	*Oblique*
Masculine	kako	kakale	koko	kodole
	kado	kadale	kodo	godole
	gado	gadale	kuko	kukule
	ko	kole	godo	
Feminine	katja	kakala	kodja	kodola
	kadja	kadala		
	gadja	gadala		
	kutja	kukula		
	koj	kola		

	These		*Those*	
	Subject	*Oblique*	*Subject*	*Oblique*
Masculine	kakale	kakale	kodole	kodole
	kole	kole	dole	dole
	kol	kol		
Feminine	kakala	kakala	kodola	kodola
	kola	kola	dola	dola

Syntactically, like adjectives and possessive pronouns, these may precede or follow the noun, and may occur together with other determiners:

kodo mas	"that meat"
o mas o kodo	"that (particular) meat"
kodo o mas	"that meat"
o mas murro	"my meat"
o mas kodo	"that (particular) meat"
o mas o murro	"my (particular) meat"
kodo murro mas	"that meat of mine"
murro mas kodo	"that meat of mine"
kodo mas murro	"that meat of mine"
o mas o kodo o murro	"that (particular) meat of mine"

Demonstratives have many functions; they can serve as conjunctions such as **kadja ke** "in order that" or adverbials such as **gadja** or **kadja** "thus, like that" and together with **sa** "all" provide the thematic translation of "(the) same:"

sa godo Rrom si k'o vudar	"the same man is at the door"
'aj tuke sa kadja!	"and the same to you!"
phiravel sa gadja còxa, voj	"she's wearing the same dress"
dja vov mange pàlpale sa kodole love	"he gave the same money back to me"

Equative comparisons (page 77) may be constructed with **sa** plus the appropriate demonstrative also:

sa gadja de bari si, sar kodja
"it is as big as that (one)"
lit. "the same of size it is, like that one"

"The same" as a noun is heard in the Serbian loanword **ìsto** in Machvano Vlax, while **mìzmo** as an adjective (from Spanish) is heard in the Arxentinicka Kalderash dialect. Other ways of expressing this are by **sa jekh (fjàlo)** "all the same" (also "it makes no difference"), **sa kodo fjàlo** "of the same kind," **jekh sas** "they were the same," &c. Yet another way to express this is with **vi...kàde: vi me kàde kerdem e butji** "I did the same work too."

The phrase **ànda** + DEM can mean either "because of that, for that reason," or "instead of," thus:

Anda kodja, me kerdem kado "instead of (doing) that, I did this"
Anda kadja, me kerdem les "for that reason, I did it"

There is one demonstrative which now only operates as a noun in Vlax, although it retains its original function in some non-Vlax dialects. This has the singular forms **kova** (masculine) and **koja** (feminine), with the masculine and feminine shared plural **kola**. It means "that person" or "that thing:"

de ma kodo kova "give me that thing"
so mangel koja? "what does she want?"
kodo koveske kher "that sort of house"

Other words for "thing" are **vàreso, pràma, trjàbo, djèli** and **djèlica; butji** "work" can mean "thing" or "affair, business."

Athematic Grammar

While it is possible to give some general rules for the morphology of athematic items, there are many exceptions, especially with the plurals of nouns, and these need to be learned separately. While athematicity is mainly determined by the category of the word itself, it is also regulated in Vlax Romani by the placement of the syllable stress. Thus the word **dorjàvo** "river," although from Persian and therefore thematic, behaves as an athematic item because it does not have final stress (its plural is **dorjàvurja**, for example, and not *__dorjave__). Similarly, the past participle derived from the initially-stressed thematic root √**kìd-** "gather" is **kidime** (rather than the expected *__kido__). The word **čelo** or **kelo** which is from Romanian on the other hand, has final stress and therefore behaves thematically. Such statements only reflect general tendencies, however, since even some thematic nouns with non-final stress, such as **lìndri** "sleep," or **čùnrra** "curl," conform to thematic grammatical rules.

Athematic Verbs

Present Tense

Athematic verbs can only take the thematic person/number suffixes if they are first added to an NFA. Otherwise, they fall into two sets, *viz.* those which take an {-i-} throughout in the person/number suffix, and those which take an {-o-}. Some examples of such verbs include:

-i- *Suffix*		-o- *Suffix*	
vol-i-l	"loves"	**ram-o-l**	"writes"
xašt-i-l	"yawns"	**farb-o-l**	"paint
kinu-i-l	"suffers"	**vest-o-l**	"notifies"
kej-i-l	"repents"	**turt-o-l**	"presses in"
fer-i-l	"protects"	**trjaz-o-l**	"sobers up"
cip-i-l	"shouts"	**šir-o-l**	"strings"
ažut-i-l	"helps"	**prič-o-l**	"says"

In the present tense these have two forms, the long, which takes thematic person/number endings, and the and short, examples of which are given above. The long form has the formula

ROOT + {-i-} *or* {-o-} + {-sar-} + PERSON/NUMBER SUFFIX.

Using **vol-i-** "love" as an *i*-verb model and **ram-o-** "write" as an *o*-verb model, the present tense is:

vol-i-sar-av	"I love"	**ram-o-sar-av**	"I write"
vol-i-sar-es	"you love"	**ram-o-sar-es**	"you write"
vol-i-sar-el	"he loves"	**ram-o-sar-el**	"he writes"
vol-i-sar-as	"we love"	**ram-o-sar-as**	"we write"
vol-i-sar-en	"you (pl.) love"	**ram-o-sar-en**	"you (pl.) write"
vol-i-sar-en	"they love"	**ram-o-sar-en**	"they write"

The short forms omit the {-sar-} and the vowel of the person/number suffix; these are commoner than the long forms:

vol-i-v[1]	vol-i-s	ram-o-v	ram-o-s
vol-i-s	vol-i-n	ram-o-s	ram-o-n
vol-i-l	vol-i-n	ram-o-l	ram-o-n

Some speakers of Lovari Vlax pronounce, and often write, the {-il} ending as /-ij/. The verb **vol-i-** "love" is also pronounced **voj-i-** by some Lovari and Kalderash speakers.

Imperative

The imperative for these verbs ends in {-sar}, which does not change for the plural:

jertisar ma   "excuse me," to one or more people
ramosar tj'o anav katka   "write your name here"

The Aorist Tense

The athematic aorist stem takes the NFA {-d-} because of the /-r-/ of the preceding {-sar-}, which must remain with the stem. There are no short aorist forms. The pattern is

ROOT + {-i-} *or* {-o-} + {-sar-} + {-d-} + P/N SUFFIX[1]:

vol-i-sar-d-em	"I loved"	**farb-o-sar-d-em**	"I wrote"
vol-i-sar-d-jan	"you loved"	**farb-o-sar-d-jan**	"you wrote"
vol-i-sar-d-ja(s)	"he loved"	**farb-o-sar-d-ja(s)**	"he wrote"
vol-i-sar-d-jam	"we loved"	**farb-o-sar-d-jam**	"we wrote"
vol-i-sar-d-jan	"you loved"	**farb-o-sar-d-jan**	"you wrote"
vol-i-sar-d-e	"they loved"	**farb-o-sar-d-e**	"they wrote"

Some athematic verbs, especially in Lovari Vlax, can take the NFA {-n-}(+{d}) instead of {-sar-}(+{-d-}) in the aorist. This is probably influence from the Central Romani dialects:

---

[1]There is also a small group of *thematic* verbs which take /-o-/ in the third person singular and plural, *e.g.* **čhav**, **thav** both "put," **thav** "wash," **xandjav** "itch" and **mothav** ~ **mothov** "speak, say," this latter historically deriving from **mo-s** (oblique of **muj** "mouth") + **thav** "put."

cip-i-l	"he shouts"
cip-i-n-d-ja	"he shouted" (beside **cipisardja**)

grop-o-l	"he digs"
grop-o-n-d-ja	"he dug" (beside **groposardja**)

tilefon-i-l	"he telephones"
tilefon-i-n-d-ja	"he telephoned" (beside **tilefonisardja**; also **tilefondja**)

This NFA also occurs in a few athematic past participles, *e.g.* **dživindime** "alive, living," alongside **dživindo**[1].

Athematic Past Participles

The athematic past participle is made by adding {**-me**} to the verb stem, *i.e.* the verb root plus accompanying vowel. The stems of √**vol-** "love" and √**farb-** "paint" are **vol-i-** and **farb-o-**:

vol-i-me	"beloved"	**farb-o-me**	"painted"
meretime	"married" (of a woman)	**skrumome**	"sooty"
ansurime	"married" (of a man)	**turtome**	"pressed in"
pokelime	"defiled"	**vestome**	"informed"
marime	"defiled"	**skucome**	"sharpened"
kulčime	"tangled"	**pahome**	"frozen
hamime	"mixed" (also **hamome**)	**(x)ramome**	"written"

These behave as adjectives, and can be inflected for gender, number and case, although many speakers use the unchanged base form (above) in all positions:

masc. sg. subject	**vol-i-me**	masc. sg. oblique	**vol-i-me-ne**
masc. pl. subject	**vol-i-me**	masc. pl. oblique	**vol-i-me-ne**
fem. sg. subject	**vol-i-me**	fem. sg. oblique	**vol-i-me-n-ja**
fem. pl. subject	**vol-i-me**	fem. pl. oblique	**vol-i-me-ne**

---

[1]The verb itself, √**dživ-** "live," which is thematic, as well as the derived nominal **dživipe(n)** "life," have been lost in Vlax, and replaced by the Rumanian-derived √**traj-** and **tràjo** respectively.

120

Ašundem murre volimene phralestar
"I heard from my beloved brother"
Kerdja les la farbomenja phalasa
"he made it with the painted plank"

Some thematic verbs take this athematic participial suffix,
e.g. **kidime** "gathered, met together" (probably because of the non-final stress of the root √kìd-), and **dživindime**, discussed above.

Verbs: Inchoatives, Causatives and Passives

There is no clearly predictable way to codify verbal behavior
in these categories. There are suffixes which produce inchoative
forms from thematic adjectival roots, and passive forms when added
to verbal roots; athematic adjective-derived inchoatives are
modelled upon athematic verb-derived passives, and sometimes,
these different forms function as reflexives. Broadly, however, they
may be divided into the two classes, thematic and athematic, each
of which has its own means of deriving the inchoative, causative,
passive and reflexive forms.

Verbs: Inchoatives: Thematic

Verbal forms called *inchoatives* may be derived from
thematic adjectives. *Inchoative* means "entering into a state of
being ~," "becoming ~," or simply "being ~:" "I'm (getting) sleepy,"
"the leaf is (turning) yellow."

a) Present

The formula for the present tense is:

THEM. ADJ. ROOT + {-j-} + {-ov-} + PRES. PERS./NUM.

Using the adjective √**bang**- "twisted, crooked" as an example,
the following inchoative verb is derived in the present tense:

bang-j-ov-av	"I am (entering into a state of being) crooked"
bang-j-ov-es	"you are (entering into a state of being) crooked"
bang-j-ov-el	"he, she, it is crooked"
bang-j-ov-as	"we are crooked"
bang-j-ov-en	"you (pl.) are crooked"
bang-j-ov-en	"they are crooked"

These NFA's, {-j-} and {-ov-}, are also used to create passives from verbal roots; this is discussed on page 125. Verbs with these NFA's have a set of common short forms also, which are more usually heard, *viz.*

STEM + {-j-} + {-o-} + PRES. PERS./NUMBER consonant ending
This is less frequently done for the first person singular:

bang-j-o-v	"I am crooked" (but more often **bangjovav**)
bang-j-o-s	"you are crooked"
bang-j-o-l	"he, she, it is crooked"
bang-j-o-s	"we are crooked"
bang-j-o-n	"you (pl.) are crooked"
bang-j-o-n	"they are crooked"

Since the second person singular and the first person plural have identical short forms, the long forms are sometimes used to disambiguate them.

Don't confuse these verbs with {-o-} with ordinary athematic verbs which also take {-o-} in the person/number suffix, such as **farbol**, **ramol**, &c. (discussed on page 117).

Some other examples:

√phur-	"old"	**phurjovel** or **phurjol**	"he gets old"
√čorr-	"poor"	**čorrjovel** or **čorrjol**	"he becomes poor"
√dil-	"stupid"	**diljovel** or **diljol**	"he becomes stupid"
√lol-	"red"	**loljoven** or **loljon**	"they turn red"
√san-	"slender"	**sanjoven** or **sanjon**	"they grow slender"
√kišl-	"thin"	**kišljovas** or **kišljos**	"we grow thin"
√tang	"narrow"	**tangjovel** or **tangjol**	"it gets narrow"
√mat-	"drunk"	**matjovel** or **matjol**	"he's getting drunk"

Note that sound changes affect some of these pronunciations: {-o-} becomes {-u-} before /v/ for a majority of speakers (**phurjovel → phurjuvel**), and a [g] before a [j] goes to a [dž] in some dialects, so that **tangjol** is pronounced (and sometimes spelt) **tandžol**. Remember too that in some dialects an [n] between an [a] and an [i] (or [j]) disappears, so that **sanjos** sounds like [**sajos**].

NB the variant forms for some speakers, which incorporate the nominal-derived inchoative NFA: **čorràvel** "I become poor," **čorrvàvol** "he becomes poor," **diljàvav** "I become stupid," **diljàvol** "he becomes stupid."

b) Imperative

The imperative retains the {-j-o} of the short form in the singular, and takes an {-n} in the plural:

kišljo!   "get thin!, lose weight!"
na matjon!   "don't get drunk!"

c) Aorist

The inchoative aorist is made thus:
ADJ. ROOT + {-i-} + {-l-} + AORIST PERS./NUMBER
Instead of {-ja(s)} for the third person singular aorist suffix, however, this is {-o} (masculine) or {-i} (feminine):

bang-i-l-em   "I became bent"
phur-i-l-em   "I got old"
čorrilo   "he grew poor"
čorrili   "she grew poor"
lolile   "they turned red"
khajliljam   "we grew lazy"

sar pašili e tàmna, šutjile 'e patrja
"as autumn drew near, the leaves began to wither"
lako muj kingilo lake asvendar
"her face grew wet from her tears"

d) Inchoatives from Nouns

i. Present

These take the stressed NFA {-àv-}:

čik	"mud"
čik-àv-	"get muddy"

bokh	"hunger"
bokh-àv-	"grow hungry"

xol-i	"anger"
xol-i-àv-	"get angry" (written <xoljav->)

ii. Imperative

In the singular, the NFA {-àv-} is retained, and followed by {-o}; in the plural, {-n} is affixed to this. The /v/ disappears in pronunciation and spelling:

na čikào! (for *čikàvo*)   "don't get muddy!," sg.
na xoljàon! (for *xoljàvon*) "don't get mad!," pl.

iii. Aorist

The aorist stem keeps the NFA {-àv-}, which retains its stress but which loses its /-v/ in pronunciation and spelling, then takes the NFAs {-i-l-} followed by the aorist NFA {-l-} (the /l/ is not written twice).
The third person is marked for gender, and {-a-i-l-} is written <-ajl->:
NOM. ROOT + {-à-} + {-i-} + {-l-} + {-l-} + PERS. NUM. SUFFIX
  xoli-à-i-l-l-o   "he got angry"   (← xoliavilo → xoljajlo)
  čik-à-i-l-l-i   "she got muddy"   (← čikavili → čikajli)
  čik-à-i-l-l-e   "they got muddy"   (← čikavile → čikajle)
Note also the imperfect and the pluperfect, which are accompanied by shift of stress to the right:

čik-av-àv-as	"I was getting muddy"
čik-av-èl-as	"he was getting muddy"
čik-a(v)-i-l-l-èm-as	"I had become muddy"

Verbs: Inchoatives: Athematic

i. Present

When the adjective root is athematic, the inchoative is formed in the same way as the passive athematic verb (page 126), *i.e.* with the NFA {-s-} before the {àv-}, thus:

| òbl-o | "round" |
| obl-o-s-àv-el | "it becomes round" |

| kòpt-o | "ripe" |
| kopt-o-s-àv-el | "it ripens" |

ii. Imperative

The imperative for passive verbs of this kind is the present inchoative stem plus {-o} for the singular, and {-on} for the plural:

| oblosàvo! | "get round!" | *cf.* oblos "you (sg.) make (something) round" |
| na djikosàvon! | "don't get wild!" | *cf.* djikon "you (pl.) make (someone) wild" |

iii. Aorist

The athematic inchoative aorist is formed from the adjectival stem (òbl-o-, kòpt-o-), which retains the NFA {-s-àv-} from the present tense, + {-i-l-} + aorist NFA {-l-} + the appropriate person/number endings. The third person is marked for gender and number, and the /v/ disappears in pronunciation and spelling (thus {-s-av-i-l-} → {-sajl-}):

obl-o-s-àv-i-l-l-em   "I grew round" (= oblosàjlem)

| obl-o-s-àv-i-l-l-o | "he got round" (= **oblosàjlo**) |
| obl-o-s-av-i-l-l-i | "she became round" (= **oblosàjli**) |

| oblosàljam | "we grew round" |
| oblosàjle | "they became round" |

oblosàjlo o kotor kašt sar strugalìvas les
"the piece of wood became round as I was planing it"

Verbs: Passives: Thematic

Passive verbs, in which the action is directed at the subject instead of the object of the sentence, are formed from the aorist stem together with the {**-j-ov-**} NFA (page 120), and the person/number suffixes:

i. Present

√ker-	"make, do"	*present root*
ker-d-	"made, did"	*aorist stem*
ker-d-j-ov-	"be made, be done"	*present passive stem*

| ker-d-j-ov-av | "I am made" (*i.e.* "I am born," *also* "I pretend") |
| ker-d-j-ov-el | "he is made" |

Also

| ker-d-j-ov-el | "he is made" (see page 121 for the short forms) |

Some thematic verbs incorporate the further NFAs {**-in-i-**} before it, for example **parru-d-in-i-s-àv-** "remake," **vazd-(-d-)-in-i-s-àv-** "arise."

ii. Imperative

The imperative is the same as the present passive stem minus {**-v-**} in the singular, with a final {**-n**} in the plural:

| kerdjo! | "pretend!" | *singular* |
| kerdjon! | "pretend!" | *plural* |

iii. Aorist

The aorist NFAs for verb-derived passives are the same as those used for the adjective-derived inchoative aorists, *viz.* {-i-l-}:

ker-d-i-l-   "was made, was done" *preterite passive stem*
ker-d-i-l-em   "I was made" (*i.e.* "I was born," "I pretended")
ker-d-i-l-o   "he was made"
ker-d-i-l-i   "she was made"

Some speakers of Russian Kalderashitska palatalize the {-d-}, pronouncing these as [**kerdjilem**], [**kerdjiljan**], &c. Speakers of Machvanitska palatalize the /k-/: [**kjerdilem**] ~ [**čerdilem**].

Verbs: Passives: Athematic

i. Present

The athematic present tense passive is constructed in accordance with the following formula:
ROOT + {-o-}/{-i-} + {-s-} + {-àv-} + PRES. PERS./NUM.
This also has short forms for the second and third persons (singular and plural) which keeps the vowel affix of the athematic stem, plus the consonant on the person/number ending:

farb-   "paint"   *verb root*
farb-o-   *present indicative stem*
farb-o-l   "he paints"
farb-o-sar-d-   *aorist stem*
farb-o-s-àv-   *present passive stem*
farb-o-s-àv-o-l "he is painted"

ii. Imperative

The imperative for passive verbs of this kind is the present passive stem plus {-o} singular, or {-o-n} plural:
farbosàvo!   "get painted!"   *cf.* **farbos** "you (sg.) paint"
na bucuisàvon! "don't get pushed!"   *cf.* **bucuin** "you (pl.) push"

iii. Aorist

The aorist tense for these verbs is made on this pattern:
STEM + {-s-} + {-àv-} {-i-} + {-l-} + {-l-} + AOR. PERS./NUM.
{-àv-i-l-} goes to {-àjl-}, and the third person singular is marked for gender.

farb-o-s-àv-i-l- (→ <**farbosàjl->**) *aorist passive stem* "was painted"

farb-o-s-àv-i-l-em	"I was painted"
farb-o-s-àv-i-l-jan	"you were painted"
farb-o-s-àv-i-l-o	"he was painted"
farb-o-s-àv-i-l-i	"she was painted"
farbosàjljam	"we were painted"
farbosàjle	"they were painted"

mir-i-	"shock, surprise (s.o.)"
mir-i-s-àv-	"be startled"

mir-i-sar-d-	"startled (s.o.)" *aorist active stem*
mir-i-s-àv-i-l-	"was startled" *aorist passive stem*

mirisardja la raklja kàna cirdja-pe pàla late
"he startled the girl when he crept up behind her"
e rakli mirisàjli kàna cirdja-pe pàla late
"the girl was startled when he crept up behind her"

Sometimes passive and inchoative forms function as reflexive verbs:

luvud-i-	"praise"
luvud-i-s-àv-	"boast," *i.e.* "praise oneself," although this is *lit.* "be praised"

Verbs: Causatives: Thematic

Causative verbs, sometimes called denominative verbs, indicate that the subject of the sentence brings an action about, *i.e.*

128

causes it to happen. This is formed in different ways, depending upon whether the root is thematic or athematic, or a verb, an adjective or a noun.

Causatives From Verbs

Causatives from thematic verbs incorporate the unstressed NFA {-av-}:

i. Present

√ačh-	"stay, wait"
ačh-av-	"cause to stay; apprehend, detain"

√dar-	"fear"
dar-av-	"cause to fear; frighten, scare"

√phand-	"close up, shut"
phand-av-	"cause to be closed up; imprison"

ii. Imperative

The imperative retains the {-av-} in the singular, to which {-en} is added in the plural:

ač**h**a*v* les othe! "keep him there!" *cf.* a**č**h othe "wait there"
na darave*n* len! "don't scare them!" *cf.* na dara*n* "don't be scared!"

iii. Aorist

In the aorist tense, the /-v-/ of the NFA {-av-} is lost, and the aorist stem NFA {-d-} is inserted:

ačhavel la raklja	"he is detaining the girl"
ačhadja la raklja	"he detained the girl"
darade 'e čhiriklen	"they frightened the birds"

Causatives From Adjectives

i. Present

Causative stems from thematic adjectives are regularly made by affixing ± {-i-} + {-ar-} (→ <-(j)ar->) to the root:

√**khamn-**	"pregnant"
khamn-i-ar-	"cause to be pregnant, impregnate"
√**tang**	"narrow"
tang-i-ar-	"cause to be narrow, make narrow"
√**mat-**	"intoxicated"
mat-i-ar-	"cause to get drunk"

ii.Imperative

The imperative keeps the (({-i-}) + {-ar} in the singular, to which {-en} is affixed in the plural:

na matjar murra cịkna pheja!
"don't get my little sister drunk!"
tangjare*n* (→ tandžare*n*) o puterdimos
"make the opening narrower"
na šudrjar amaro xabe; phandav e filjàstra!
"don't make our food (get) cold; close the window!"

iii. Aorist

The aorist retains the present stem, which is followed by the aorist stem NFA {-d-}:

matjar-d-ja	"he caused (s.o.) to be drunk"
kaljarde penge fèciji	"they blackened-up their faces"
kovljardem o mom	"I softened the wax"
tatjardjam o paj	"we heated the water"

Causatives From Nouns

i. Present

Causatives derived from thematic nouns are not common; the structural sequence is NOMINAL ROOT + {-(j)ar-}:

drab	"medicine"	**rjat**	"night"
drab-ar-	"divine, predict fate"	**ratjar-**	"spend the night"

xol-	"anger"	**čik**	"mud"
xol-i-ar-	"cause to be angry"	**čik-ar-**	"cause to be muddy"

Cf. also √**xoljak-** "angry," √**čikal-** "muddy," and the inchoatives **xoljàv-** "get angry" and **čikàv-** "get muddy" (see previous page).

ii. Imperative

{-(j)-ar-} is kept in the singular, to which {-en} is suffixed in the plural:

na čikar le vast	"don't get your hands muddy"
na xoljaren kodole guruves	"don't make that bull mad"

iii. Aorist

This is formed in the same way as the adjectives, above: **čikardem** ~ "I made ~ muddy," **čikardjan amari ponjàva tjire kherandar** "you made our carpet muddy with (= from) your boots."

Verbs from Prepositions

Verbs can be made from some prepositions employing the same suffixes as those which derive them from adjectives or nouns:

pàš-a	"near"	**tèl-a**	"down"
paš-jo-v-	"draw near, approach"	**tel-j-ar-**	"set out, leave"
paš-jo-v-el	"he draws near, approaches"	**tel-j-ar-el**	"he sets off"

Also
  paš-j-o-l
  paš-i-l-o   "he approached"   **tel-j-ar-d-ja** "he set off"

NB the similar **paš-l-j-ov-** "lie down," **paš-l-j-ar-** "lay s.t. down, put to bed." *NB* also the difference between the present participle forms **pašindoj** "getting closer" and **pašlindoj** "lying down."

A List of Derived Verbs

ampęčisar-	"settle someone's argument"
ampęčisàv-	"be mollified, reconciled"
ankęr-	"hold s.t."
ankęrdjov-	"calm down, get a grip on o.s."
anklj-	"climb up on"
anklav-	"remove, pull out, poke out, extract"
ansurisar-	"marry a male person to s.o. else"
ansurisàv-	"(for a man to) get married"
ansučisar-	"twist something"
ansučisàv-	"get twisted"
arakh-	"find, guard, take care of"
arakhàdjov-	"meet; be born"
astar-	"catch; fasten together, grip"
astàrdjov-	"cling onto, fasten onto"
ažutisar-	"help"
ažutisàv-	"fend for oneself; manage"
barjov-	"grow, get bigger"
barvàv-	"get rich"

baš-	"produce noise; play an instrument; bark"
bašav-	"make a noise with something"
bįzęjisar-	"stir, mix, rake, poke"
bįzęjisàv-	"interfere, get involved in"
bolisar-	"make s.o. ill"
bolisàv-	"get sick"
bụster-	"forget"
bụsterdjov-	"be forgotten"
bušluisar-	"make someone sad"
bušluisàv-	"grow sad"
buxlar-	"widen, make s.t. wider"
buxljov-	"grow wider, broader"
cępęnisar-	"stiffen s.t., make s.t. stiff"
cępęnisàv-	"grow stiff, stiffen up"
cįnjar-	"make smaller, diminish"
cįnjov-	"grow smaller, shrink"
čhin-	"cut"
čhinav-	"intend, decide, make an offer"
čhor-	"pour, spill"
čhordjov-	"get spilt, overflow"
dara-	"be afraid"
darav-	"frighten someone"
dikh-	"look, see"
dikhjov-	"appear, seem, be regarded"
diljar-	"dupe s.o."
diljàv-	"go crazy"

domolisar-	"quieten s.o. down"
domolisàv-	"grow quiet"
drĭnčinisar-	"shake"
drĭnčinisàv-	"be shaken up"
dukha-	"ache"
dukhàv-	"cause pain"
durjar-	"send away"
durjov-	"go away"
garav-	"conceal s.t., hide s.t."
garadjov-	"hide o.s."
gelbenisar-	"paint s.t. yellow"
gelbenisàv-	"turn yellow"
getisar-	"prepare, make s.t. ready"
getisàv-	"get o.s. ready"
gindisar-	"think, suppose"
gindisàv-	"imagine, conceive"
grebisar-	"hurry s.o. up"
grebisàv-	"be in a hurry"
hamisar-	"mix, stir, agitate"
hamisàv-	"be involved, interfere, meddle"
hulav-	"share, divide"
huladjov-	"part from, separate from"
inčerežisar-	"interest, make interested"
inčerežisàv-	"be interested"
kenterisar-	"weigh, be heavy"
kenterisàv-	"weigh s.t., balance s.t."

kịlčisar-	"tangle s.t. up"
kịlčisàv-	"get confused, get muddled up"
kirav-	"cook s.t."
kirjov-	"be cooking, be getting cooked"
kovljar-	"soften s.t. up, make s.t. soft"
kovljov-	"grow soft"
kunuisar-	"marry two people"
kunuisàv-	"get married to s.o."
khajljar-	"feed, nourish"
khajljov-	"become sated, full, replete"
lang-	"limp"
langàv-	"grow lame"
langjov-	"cripple s.o."
lęgnisar-	"rock, swing s.t., s.o."
lęgnisàv-	"waddle, sway, be dangling"
lịpisar-	"stick s.t. to s.t."
lịpisàv-	"be stuck together"
lụngjar-	"extend, lengthen"
lụngjov-	"grow longer"
malav-	"beat, strike, make contact with"
maladjov-	"encounter, meet"
mar-	"beat, strike, make contact with"
mardjov-	"ring (as a telephone)"
matjar-	"get s.o. drunk"
matjov-	"become intoxicated"

mẹcisar-	"stun"
mẹcisàv-	"pass out"
merisar-	"bother s.o."
merisàv-	"worry about s.t."
mẹrẹtisar-	"marry off a daughter"
mẹrẹtisàv-	"(for a girl to) get married"
morcosar-	"make s.t. numb"
morcosàv-	"lose feeling"
mucosar-	"cause to be speechless"
mucosàv-	"grow dumb"
mučisar-	"move s.t."
mučisàv-	"move o.s."
nakh-	"cross over, pass by, happen"
nakhav-	"carry over, send, transfer"
nangjar-	"undress s.o."
nangjov-	"get undressed"
naš-	"flee, elope"
našav-	"abduct, elope with; send; swallow"
nẹbušisar-	"make s.o. sweat"
nẹbušisàv-	"sweat"
nẹkẹžisar-	"make sad or anxious"
nẹkẹžisàv-	"grow sad or anxious"
oblosar-	"make round, smooth the edges of"
oblosàv-	"become round"
pahosar-	"freeze s.t."
pahosàv-	"freeze, congeal, feel cold, get frozen"

136

parruv-	"exchange; replace s.t."
parrudjov-	"be changed, become altered"
parrudinisàv-	"alter, remake s.t."
pašjar-	"lay s.t. down"
pašljov-	"lie down"
patja-	"obey, respect"
patjav-	"believe, trust"
pẹr-	"fall, drop down"
pẹrav-	"drop, let fall"
phabar-	"singe, set fire to"
phabjov-	"be on fire, be burning"
phag-	"break s.t."
phagjov-	"come apart, get broken"
phànd-	"shut, tie up"
phandav-	"shut s.o. up, imprison"
phandadjov-	"shut itself, *e.g.* of a door"
pharruv-	"die, of an animal"
pharrav-	"divide, share"
pharradjov-	"split into pieces"
phẹr-	"fill s.t. up"
phẹrdjov-	"get full"
phir-	"walk"
phirav-	"lead about, guide"
phučar-	"widen, make broader"
phučjov-	"swell, bulge, expand"
phurjar-	"make s.t., s.o. old"
phurjov-	"grow old"

podisar-	"mess s.t. up"
podisàv-	"get untidy"
podjisar-	"shoe s.o., s.t., *e.g.* a horse"
podjisàv-	"put one's own shoes on"
pornisar-	"get something started"
pornisàv-	"start off, set out"
porrav-	"devour hungrily; wolf down food; open wide; deflower"
porràdjov-	"stretch"
potopisar-	"drown s.o."
potopisàv-	"get drowned, be drowning"
prępędisar-	"kill, destroy, maim"
prępędisàv-	"succumb, be destroyed"
prikęzisar-	"cause bad luck to"
prikęzisàv-	"have bad luck"
p(r)indžar-	"recognise"
p(r)indžardjov-	"introduce o.s."
putr-	"open something, undo, untie"
puterdjov-	"become undone"
rimosar-	"destroy, ruin, damage"
rimosàv-	"get damaged"
rrętęčisar-	"mislead, lead astray"
rrętęčisàv-	"go astray, get lost"
rrugjisar-	"entreat, beg, beseech"
rrugjisàv-	"pray to"

sęmnosar-	"mark, designate"
sęmnosàv-	"get marked, be designated"
sikav-	"demonstrate, indicate, point out s.t."
sikadjov-	"show o.s., appear; haunt"
sikjov-	"learn, teach o.s."
sikjar-	"teach, instruct, educate"
skępisar-	"set free"
skępisàv-	"escape"
skurcar-	"shorten s.t."
skurcjov-	"grow short, shrink"
sov-	"sleep"
sovljar-	"put to sleep, lull"
šęžosar-	"squeeze s.t."
šęžosàv-	"get squeezed, be crushed"
šukjar-	"dry s.t."
šukjov-	"get dry, become dehydrated"
tangjar-	"make narrow"
tangjov-	"grow narrow"
tasàdjov-	"choke, suffocate (o.s.)"
tasav-	"choke, suffocate, strangle s.o."
tasuv-	"choke, suffocate, drown (o.s.)"
tatjar-	"heat s.t. up"
tatjov-	"get hot"
tęrdjar-	"stop s.t."
tęrdjov-	"stop o.s., come to a halt, pull up"
tęvęlisar-	"roll s.t."
tęvęlisàv-	"roll o.s. about, wallow"

thuljar-	"thicken s.t., fatten s.t. up"
thuljov-	"grow thick, grow fat"
vačisar-	"complain"
vačisàv-	"complain," same as *vačisar-*
vàzd-	"lift, raise s,t., pick up s.t."
vazdinisàv-	"arise, raise o.s."
vẹsẹlisar-	"cheer s.o. up"
vẹsẹlisàv-	"rejoice, cheer up o.s."
vortosar-	"correct, set aright"
vortosàv-	"improve o.s."
votrejisar-	"poison s.o."
votrejisàv-	"be poisoned"
vuluisar-	"wrap s.t., wind up s.t."
vuluisàv-	"wrap o.s. up"
vučar-	"elevate"
vučjov-	"grow taller"
zalisar-	"knock s.o. out"
zalisàv-	"sprain o.s."
zorjar-	"strengthen s.t., reinforce s.t."
zorjàv-	"grow strong"

Reflexive Verbs

Reflexive verbs bring the action back to the subject of the verb. In English, this is indicated by using the appropriate possessive pronouns with -*self*, thus "I wash myself," "you cut yourself," &c. In Romani, the reflexive construction is used far more than it is in English; furthermore, it sometimes conveys quite

Verbs in	Imperative Singular	Imperative Plural	Aorist NFA	Past Participle
1 {-j-ov-}	{-jo}	{-jon}	{-il-}	{-il(in)-}
2 {-(j)ar-}	{(j)ar}	{(j)aren}	{-(j)ard-}	{-(j)ard-}
3 {-av-}	{-av}	{-aven}	{-ad-}	{-ad-}
4 {-àv-}	{-àvo}	{-àvon}	{-ajl-}	{-ajl-}
5 {-sàv-}	{-sàvo}	{-sàvon}	{-sàjl-}	{-sàjl-}
6 {-sar-}	{-sar}	{-sar}	{-sard-}	{-i-/-o- + -me}

Figure 7: MORPHOLOGY OF DERIVED VERBS

1. Inchoatives from thematic verbs; passives from thematic verbs. 2. Causatives from thematic adjectives. 3. Causatives from thematic verbs; causatives from thematic nouns. 4. Inchoatives from thematic nouns. 5. Inchoatives from thematic adjectives; passives from athematic verbs. 6. Stems from athematic verbs.

a different meaning from its non-reflexive form, thus **džanav** means "I know," while **džana'-ma** means "I confess;" **patjal** means "he respects," while **patjal-pe** means "he believes;" **haljerel** means "he understands," while **haljerel-pe** means "he feels;" **phiravel** "he walks," **arakhel** "he finds" and **ankerdjovav** "he grips" all mean "he behaves" when made reflexive. Note that the /-v/ of the first person singular person/number suffix is lost before the following **ma(n)**, and that reflexive pronouns are hyphenated with their verb.

The reflexive pronouns are listed on page 62. For some speakers, the third person singular reflexive pronoun *pe* has become generalized for all persons (see note on page 62).

arakhel-pe	"he watches out; he behaves," *cf.* **arakh-** "find"
biril-pe	"it measures up, is worthy," *cf.* **bir-i-** "be able"
čhàdel-pe	"he vomits"
čhol[1]**-pe**	"he enters," *cf.* **čh-** "put"
čhùdel-pe	"he kicks" *cf.* **čhùd-** "throw"
del-pe	"he surrenders; he gives in; he enters" *cf.* **d-** "give"
doril-pe	"he misses, he pines for"
džal-pe	"it goes, it happens, it progresses" *cf.* **dž-** "go"
džuvindil-pe	"he revives, comes to"
fumol-pe	"it smokes" (*i.e.* "gives off smoke")
gindil-pe	"he thinks"
kerel-pe	"it happens" *cf.* **ker-** "do"
khelel-pe	"he dances" *cf.* **khel-** "play"
litjol-pe	"he's had enough!" *cf.* **litj-** "get crushed, mashed"
marel-pe	"he gets, he obtains" *cf.* **mar-** "beat"
morel-pe	"he loiters" *cf.* **mor-** "rub"
mukhel-pe	"it begins, it starts" *cf.* **mukh-** "let"
ramol-pe	"he autographs, signs"
rrẹpẹzil-pe	"he rushes"
rrugjil-pe	"he prays"
skrijil-pe	"he autographs, signs"
sovel-pe	"he sleeps"

---

[1]This thematic verb, whose primary meaning is "place, put, set, plant (seeds)," has the present tense conjugation **čhav, čhos, čhol, čhos, čhon, čhon**. Its imperative is **čhu** (sg.), **čhon** (pl.), aorist stem **čhut-**.

thol pe   "he enters; he begins" *cf.* **th-** "put"
xlel[1] **pe**   "he defecates"

či birisardja-pe, amari vrjàmja and'e Amèrika
"Our time in America didn't meet our expectations"

Similar to the reflexive construction are verbs which are accompanied by nominal and pronominal forms with the dative postposition, thus **xal peske** "he eats." These are discussed on page 87. Some verbs may occur in the reflexive or the dative form: **sova'-ma** or **sovav mange** "I sleep."

The Oratorical Register

There is a particular style of speaking Romani, which is used in certain dignified social contexts such as speech-making, and which may sometimes also be heard preserved in songs. This type of Romani is characterized by the use of grammatical endings on words which would not otherwise require them in ordinary speech; for example, the present indicative verb forms take a final {-a} throughout, a construction found in ordinary non-Vlax dialects and in the Vlax future tense construction (page 99), thus **dikhav** "I see," **dikhàva** "I shall see," &c.

Another feature is the use of inflected forms for adjectives and pronouns which copy those of the nouns they follow, for example when an adjective is in the predicate position. Compare **le lačhe čheja** "the good girls" with the usual **le čheja si lačhe** "the girls are good," and oratorical **le čheja si lačhja**, or **me čhindem les murra čhurjasa** "I cut it with my knife" with **me čhindem les la čhurjasa la murrasa**. These may be modelled upon Slavic grammatical patterns, or else be retentions from a once more uniform Romani grammar before it fragmented into regional dialects; forms like these are found in *e.g.* Sinti, indicating that they might have once been more common in Vlax than they are now.

---

[1]This thematic verb has the present tense conjugation **xlja'-ma, xli-tu, xlel-pe, xljas-amen, xlen-tumen, xlen-pen**. Its imperative is **xli** (sg.) and **xlen** (pl.), and the aorist stem is **xind-**.

Cf. also

avilem le kherestar le barestar
"I came from the big house"
dem les le Rromenge la Kanadakirenge
"I gave it to the Canadian Rom"
dikhela la da le Rromeskirja
"he sees the man's mother"
geljam le čhavenca la Vinkakirenca
"we went with Vinka's children"
sàko šarela peskirja
"everyone praises is own"
sa asterdjam amengirja
"we all caught our own"
peskira phejatar la ternjatar
"from his young sister"
lengiro bàjero
"their amulet"
Rromnìjo ba phurìjo!
"Hey, old lady!"
bešava le čhaveste murreste le maj phureste
"I am staying at my eldest son's (place)"

Nouns and Verbs from Other Parts of Speech

It has already been shown on page 104 how Romani can make adverbs from adjectives by adding {-es} to the thematic root. Other parts of speech can be made from words in different form classes (parts of speech) as well; for example, nouns can be made from verbs, adverbs, prepositions and so on.

The Nominalizing Suffixes {-pe} and {-mos}

The thematic suffix {-i-pe(n)} or {-i-be(n)} can be affixed to a verbal or adjectival root to create the corresponding noun, thus:

√ker-	"do, make"	√xa-	"eat"	šaj	"able"
keripe	"action"	xabe	"food"	šajipe	"ability"

√**bar-**	"big"	**šukar**	"beautiful"	√**sast-**	"healthy"
baripe	"size"	**šukaripe**	"beauty"	**sastipe**	"health"

√**s-**	"be"	**našti**	"cannot"	**mùsaj**	"must"
isipe	"existence"	**naštipe**	"inability"	**musajipe**	"necessity"

The athematic equivalent of {**-i-pe(n)**} is {**-i-mos**}. It occurs extensively in Kalderash especially, which has few nouns derived thematically (examples are **sastipe** "health" and **xabe(n)** "food," beside **sastimos** and **xaimos**). Speakers of Lovari Vlax pronounce and write this as {**-i-mo**}, while speakers in eastern Hungary and northern Romania have collapsed {**-i-pe**} and {**-i-mo**} into {**-i-po**}; in some Albanian and Macedonian Romani dialects, it is {**-i-pa**}. There is a tendency to generalize the thematic and the athematic nominalizing suffixes, *i.e.* {**-i-pe**} no longer goes exclusively with thematic roots, or {**-i-mos**} with athematic. Examples with the latter include

Adjective		*Verb*		*Adverb*	
√**cìv-**	"clever"	√**ansur-i-**	"marry"	**nìči**	"no"
civimos	"cleverness"	**ansurimos**	"marriage"	**ničimos**	"negation"

Nouns in both {**-i-pe**} and {**-i-mos**} are all masculine.

In non-Vlax Romani dialects, {**-i-pe(n)**}/{**-i-be(n)**} have plurals in {**-a**}, with syncopated ({**-bna**}). This has been lost entirely in Vlax, which employs all of the non-singular subject case morphology belonging to {**-i-mos**}. An even earlier thematic distinction, which nominalized adjectives with {**-i-pe(n)**} and verbs with {**-i-be(n)**} has also been lost.

The morphology for both suffixes is:

Subject plural	{**-i-màta**}
Oblique singular	{**-i-màs-**}
Oblique plural	{**-i-matàn-**}

Examples are:

kidimos	"meeting" (< thematic √**kìd-** "gather")
pìjipe, pìpe	"a drink" (< √**pi-**)
kidimàta	"meetings"
pimàta	"drinks"

le kidimàstar	"from the meeting"
le pimàstar	"from the drink"
le kidimatàndar	"from the meetings"
le pimatàndar	"from the drinks"

These nominalizing suffixes are being used productively in the development of the new standard dialect, with such neologisms as **kaverfjalimàta** "differences," **avimos** "realization " (*vs.* **aresajipe** "arrival"), &c., turning up in print with increasing frequency. The standardized grammar retains both suffixes (as well as a number of others listed on page 151*ff.*), using each to distinguish related concepts semantically, thus **džanglipe** "knowledge," **džanglimos** "awareness."

Athematic Vocatives

For masculine singular nouns with non-final stress, these are usually made by affixing {-òna}/{-àna} or {-òne}/{-àne} to the nominal (or nominalized adjectival) root. There are no corresponding plural vocative suffixes:

kolègo "colleague" **dràgo** "beloved" **Stèvo** "Stephen"
kolegòna! "oh colleague!" **dragòna!** "oh dear one!" **Stevàne!** "oh Stephen!"

For feminine singular nouns in {-(j)-a}, an {-o} is added to the root. There is no special plural vocative suffix; the subject case forms are used instead:

fìna "god-daughter" **vùlpja** "fox" **Àna** "Anne"
fìno! "oh god-daughter!" **vùlpjo** "oh fox!" **Àno** "oh Anne!"

There many vocative forms in Romani, especially for kinship terms. Some of these include:

bàči	"sir!"
bre	"sir!"
dadìka	"dear father!" (*them.*)

dàjka	"sister-in-law!"
dòjka	"sister-in-law!"
dragòno	"dear one!" (for **dragòna**)
kẹtàno	"soldier!"
krẹcùle	"curly!" (*cf.* **krèco** "curl")
màjči	"mother!, old lady!"
màjka	"mother!, old lady!"
mo, more	"sir!"
nàjka	"mother!, old lady!"
nàna	"uncle!"
njànja	"aunty!"
nòno	"uncle!"
Orxàne	"hey Orhan!" (proper male name)
Perxàne	"hey Perhan!" (proper male name)
sokròna	"father-in-law!"
Stevàne	"hey Steve!" (proper male name)
šukarène	"beautiful one!" (*them.*)
šukarìja	"beautiful one!" (*them.*; for **šukarìjo**)
tàjka	"little boy!"

Athematic Adjectives

In the subject case, athematic adjectives are inflected for number but not for gender, although gender is marked in the singular oblique case. Using **pròsto** "ordinary" as a model, the regular athematic suffixes are as follows:

	Singular	*Plural*
Masculine and Feminine Subject	**pròst-o**	**prost-o-n-e**
Masculine Oblique	**pròst-i**	**prost-o-n-e**
Feminine Oblique	**prost-o-n-ja**	**prost-o-n-e**

The thematic item **kuč** "dear" takes the above athematic morphology.

There are dozens of irregular athematic adjectives, which have different forms in the subject plurals. A few of these include:

Subject sg.	Subject pl.	
anglizìcko	anglizìcka	"English" (see page 163)
ạntrègo	ạntrèži	"entire"
càpẹno	càpẹnja	"stiff"
cịvo	cịvi	"clever"
dràgo	dràži	"beloved"
djìko	djìki	"wild, crude"
gàtạ	gẹ̀ci	"ready"
hàrniko	hàrniči	"hardworking"
lẹnìvo	lẹnìva	"lazy"
mùčedo	mùčezi	"moldy, rancid"
slòbodo	slòbozi	"free"
stịngo	stịnži	"left (side)"
strèjno	strèja	"foreign"
vurrìto	vurrìci	"disgusting"

Athematic Adverbs

Athematic adverbs are formed by inserting the NFA {-n-} before the thematic suffix {-es}:

mùndr-o   "attractive"
mundr-o-n-ès   "attractively"

It is not necessary to change athematic adjectives into their corresponding adverbial forms. **Gilàbal mùndro** and **gilàbal mundrones** "she sings nicely"[1] are both correct.

Athematic Nouns

Most masculine athematic nouns in the subject case consist of the root plus an unstressed final {-o} in the singular, and form their plurals by affixing {-ùrja} (as well as {-ùja}, {-ùra}, {-ùri}), also

---

[1]Note that **vòrta gilàbal**, literally "she sings right," is an idiom, and means in fact "she sings badly." "She sings well" is expressed as **gilàbal and'o muj**.

very commonly {-**ùlja**}[1], and in the oblique case take {-**os**} and an {-**on**} on the stem for the singular and plural respectively. The model is **kòto** "corner" (note shift of stress in the oblique case to syllable-final position):

	Subject	*Oblique*
Masculine Singular	o kòt-o	le kot-ò-s
Masculine Plural	le kòt-urja	le kot-ò-n

Feminine singular athematic nouns ending in an {-**i**} in the subject case usually change this to an {-**a**} in the plural while those ending in an {-**a**} in the singular change this to an {-**i**}. Using **djèla** "thing" and **kavàdji** "overcoat" as examples of each, the feminine endings are:

	Subject	*Oblique*
Feminine Singular	e djèl-a	la djel-à
	e kavàdj-i	la kavadj-à
Feminine Plural	le djèl-i	le djel-è-n
	le kavàdj-a	le kavadj-à-n

Note that in the oblique case, a shift of stress accompanies the change in suffixes[2].

Nouns in {-*no*}

Many athematic masculine singular nouns which end in a stressed vowel plus {-**no**}, pluralize this by changing that suffix to {-**ja**}:

---

[1] This plural ({-**ùlja**}) is especially common in American Kalderash. It has also been noted in Paspati (1870:439).
[2] This is also the rule for thematic items with non-final stress, *e.g.* **sàstrì** "iron," **čùnrra** "braid."

i. With -a-

aroplàno	"airplane"	aroplàja
Čajnimàno	"Oriental person"	Čajnimàja
dutjàno	"shop"	dutjàja
dušmàno	"enemy"	dušmàja
jorgàno	"cover, cloth"	jorgàja
Mačvàno	"Machvano man"	Mačvàja
Mesikàno	"Mexican man"	Mesikàja
tobolacijàno	"auctioneer"	tobolacijàja
voroslàno	"elephant"	voroslàja

ii. With -e-

džàmeno	"twin"	džamèja

iii. With -o-

izvòno	"bell"	izvòja
pantalòno	"trousers"	pantalòja
pelivòno	"wrestler"	pelivòja
plapòno	"counterpane"	plapòja
tilefòno	"telephone"	tilefòja
vizòno	"mink"	vizòja

iv. With -u-

pavùno	"peacock"	pavùja

Some nouns have alternative plurals, with those in {-ùrja} apparently replacing the above forms, e.g. fistàno "skirt, dress" has both fistàja and fistànurja, zakòno "law" has both zakòja and zakònurja, and mamùno "monkey" has both mamùja and mamùn-urja, the first being increasingly used as a singular.

The nominal oblique case is formed by adding the suffixes {-o-s} and {-o-n} to the root in the singular and plural respectively:

Mačvàn-	"Machvano"
o Mačvàno dikhlja man	"The Machvano man saw me"
dikhlem 'e Mačvànos	"I saw the Machvano man"
de les le Mačvanoske	"Give it to the Machvano man"
le Mačvàja dikhle man	"The Machvano men saw me"
dikhlem 'e Mačvànon	"I saw the Machvano men"
de len le Mačvanònge	"Give them to the Machvano men"

A number of other nouns in this category do not have matching vowels in the suffix, e.g. miljòno "million" has miljàja,

limòno "lemon" has **limùja,** which is sometimes used for the singular.

Nouns in {*-aj*}

Both thematic and athematic nouns which end in {**-aj**} sometimes make their plural by dropping the final /-**j**/:

balaj	"trough"	**bala**
bordjaj	"shackle"	**bordja**
phabaj	"apple"	**phaba**
rašaj	"holy man"	**raša**
taxtaj	"tumbler"	**taxta**

But *cf.* **kišaj** "sand," **hakaj** "right," **košaj** "cabbage stalk," **čerxaj** "star," with their plurals in {**-ja**}.

Nouns with a final /-**j**/ following other vowels, keep the /-**j**/: **buboj** "abcess," **šošoj** "rabbit," **paxoj** "ice," **taloj** "palate," **khoj** "suet," **gunoj** "garbage," **heroj** "leg," **vuloj** "oil," **morroj** "apparition," **guj** "sausage," **fusuj** "bean," **gutuj** "quince," **kukuj** "bump," **xuxuj** "wolf" (or "evil monster") &c.

Irregular Nouns

There are very many nouns whose subject plurals differ from the patterns given above, or which do not take the expected suffixes. Some examples of these include:

Masculine

alxìre	"pope"	**alxirèji**
arìče	"porcupine"	**aričèji**
barjàko	"flag"	**barjàči**
bejàto	"boy"	**bejèci**
dàrro	"gift"	**dàrrja** or **dàrrurja**
gàlbeno	"gold coin"	**gàlbi**
Këldëràš	"Kalderash"	**Këldëràša**
kòkalo	"bone"	**kòkala**
kokòšo	"rooster"	**kokòša**
kòlo	"circle, group"	**kòlja**

kopàči	"treetrunk"	**kopàča**
mobìli	"car"	**mobìlja**
pęrìnto	"ancestor"	**pęrìnci**
pohàro	"tumbler"	**pohàri**
praznìco	"holiday"	**praznikìči**
sęnisèro	"ashtray"	**sęnisèrja**
sitjàri	"teacher"	**sitjàrja**
tòpo	"cannon"	**tòpi** or **tòpurja**
vortàko	"partner"	**vortàča**
Feminine		
bjàrja	"beer"	**bèri**
blùdka	"saucer"	**blùdi**
čireš	"cherry"	**čireša**
dàta	"occasion"	**dèci**
dràma	"drama"	**drèmi**
> **ketàna**	"soldier"	**ketàja** or **ketàna**
khelitòrka	"dancer"	**khelitòrki**
màrja	"sea"	**mèri**
pàrtja	"part"	**pèrci**
ponjàva	"carpet"	**ponjèvi**
rrobìja	"jail"	**rrobìji**
sitjàrka	"teacher"	**sitjàrki**
šàtra	"canopy"	**šętri**
vàrga	"stripe"	**vęrdži**
vjàstja	"report"	**vęsti**

The morphology for some of these categories of masculine and feminine nouns is given in the following section.

The English loan **tùlzurja** "tools" and the Machvanitska **stèpsa** "ladder" (in Kalderashitska **skàra**) both have double plurals, incorporating the English {-s}.

Lexical Modification by Prefix and Suffix

Other parts of speech, as well as different shades of meaning attached to the same part of speech, can be achieved by employing various suffixes with the lexical roots and stems, some of which (*e.g.*

{-i-pe}, {-i-mos}, {-tar}) have been discussed already. These seem to be used in a general way with particular types of words, so that *e.g.* {-(v)-al-o} is affixed to body-part names, and so on. The principal word-building suffixes include:

{-àcija}	Corresponds to {-*tion*} in English in international vocabulary items: **nàcija** "nation" **federàcija** "federation" **generàcija** "generation"
{-al}	See page 105.
{-al-}	This may be related to the following, since [v] can weaken and disappear in Romani. It forms adjectives denoting physical or moral states: **vuštalo** "having fat lips" **(o vušt** "lip") **bokhalo** "hungry" **(e bokh** "hunger") **bulali** "fat-bottomed" **(e bul** "posterior") **manušalo** "masculine" **(o manuš** "man") **patjivalo** "honorable" **(e patjiv** "esteem") **trušalo** "thirsty" **(e truš** "thirst") **zoralo** "strong" **(e zor** "power")
{-(v)-al-}	This makes adjectives which describe characteristics associated with parts of the body, thus: **čhorvalo** "bearded" **(o čhor** "beard") **čučivali** "large-breasted" **(e čuči** "breast") **nakhvalo** "big-nosed" **(o nakh** "nose") **porrvalo** "intestinal" **(e porr** "guts") **ratvalo** "bloody" **(o rat** "blood") **xandžuvalo** "stingy" **(√xandž-** "itch") *Cf.* Also **barvalo** "rich" **(√bar-** "big")
{-àra}	See page 107. This is discussed in Sampson (1926,§217), who makes a connection with {-var} (page 165) (< Sanskrit *vāra*, *cf.* Hindi *bār*).

{-àr-i}	A masculine nominal agentive suffix, indicating the doer of an action, animate or inanimate. The plural is formed with {-àrja}, and the feminine with {-àrka}, vocative with {-j-àr-i-na}:

cirdàri	"drawer"	(√cìrd- "pull")
Čuràri	"a nation of Rom"	(< Rom. *ciurar* "seive")
lavutàri	"violinist"	(e lavùta "violin")
Lovàri	"a nation of Rom"	(< Hung. *ló* "horse")
masàri	"butcher"	(o mas "meat")
paramičàri	"storyteller"	(e paramìči "story")
sastimàri	"physician"	(√sast- "healthy")
šonkàri	"pork butcher"	(o šònko "ham")
vastàri	"handle"	(o vast "hand")
vazdàri	"elevator, lift"	(√vazd- "raise")

{-aš}
{-ač(i)}
{-iš}
{-oš}
{-uš}

A masculine nominal agentive suffix, indicating the doer of an action, or the individual or thing otherwise associated with it. The plural of {-aš} is {-àša}, the feminine singular is with {-ašànka}, and the vocative is with {-ìn-a}:

bajaš	"type of non-Rom Gypsy"	(< Rom. *boiar*)
birtaš	"bartender"	(o bìrto "saloon")
buntaš	"troublemaker"	(e bùna "rebellion")
cęgaš	"marksman"	(√cęgo- "take aim")
čhibaš	"linguist"	(e čhib "language")
dutjanaš	"shopkeeper"	(o dutjàno "shop")
gàlbenuš	"yolk of an egg"	(gàlben- "yellow")
gitaraš	"guitarist"	(e gitàra "guitar")
Kęldęraš	"a nation of Rom"	(< Rom. *căldare* "kettle")
klinčìš, klinčoš	"bolt"	(< Serbian)
kočaš	"coach driver"	(< Hungarian)
koperìš	"roof"	(< Romanian)
kovàči	"blacksmith"	(< Hungarian)
lavutaš	"violinist"	(e làvuta "violin")
lękętuš	"locksmith"	(o lękęto "padlock")
patikàroš	"druggist"	(e pàtika "drugstore")
patretaš	"photographer"	(o patrèto "picture")
pęgubaš	"victim"	(e pagùba "damage")

rrobijaš	"slave-driver"	(**e rrobìja** "slavery")[1]
stingaš	"left-hander"	(√**stìng-** "left")
svataš	"spokesman"	(**o svàto** "discourse")
tolmač	"interpreter"	(√**tolmač-** "translate")
vatraš	"camp leader"	(**e vàtra** "camp)

{-a-n-} This forms adjectives which have the properties of something animate:

guruvano	"bullish, bovine"	(**o guruv** "bull)
manušano	"manly"	(**o manuš** "man")
muršano	"masculine"	(**o murš** "man")
Rromano	"Gypsy"	(**o Rrom** "Gypsy")

{-(v)-an-} Probably related to the above, and having the same function:

čorrovano	"like a poor person"	(√**čorr-** "poor")
dilivano	"like a foolish person"	(√**dil-** "foolish")

{-a-nd}
{-e-nd} This is an uncommon suffix, which makes semantically
{-i-nd} related nouns from other nouns or adjectives:

berand	"horizontal tent pole"	(**o bero** "boat"?)
ivend	"winter"	(**o iv** "snow")
pharind	"mattress"	(√**phar-** "heavy")
purrand	"foot of the bed"	(**o punrro** "foot")
šerand	"pillow, cushion"	(**o šero** "head")

{-asl-} Conveys the quality or characteristic of a noun to the adjective:

balaslo	"hairy"	(**e bal** "hair")
grumujaslo	"uneven (ground)"	(**o grumoroj** "heap")
gunojaslo	"trashy, rubbishy"	(**o gunoj** "garbage")
pajaslo	"watery"	(**o paj** "water")
phugnjalo	"spotty"	(**e phugni** "pimple")
plajinaslo	"hilly"	(**e plajin** "hill")
šeljaslo	"freckled; scurvy"	(**šelja** "freckles; dandruff")

---

[1]In American Vlax, this word means "prison."

{bi-}	See page 70.

{-èšti}   A nominal suffix indicating the name of a **vìca** or clan. Listed here are various *nacìji* with their principal clan or clans:

Arxentìnurja	**Kunèšti**
Čuràra	**Pepèšti**
Grèkurja	**Pupèšti**
Lovàra	**Bašnèšti, Imrèšti, Pulikèšti, Šandorèšti**
Mačvàja	**Kolèšti, Mòlešti**
Mesikàja	**Bokùr'šti, Čokùr'šti, Jonkùr'šti**
Rrùsurja	**Čukurèšti, Dorèšti, Djajkèšti, Frinkulèšti, Gunèšti, Gurèšti, Jocùr'šti, Mačolèšti, Ristùr'šti, Vankùr'šti**
Serbàja	**Lamèšti, Tutèšti**

{-gòdi}   Although this is treated as a suffix because of the way words containing it are written, *e.g.* **sogòdi, kongòdi, kanagòdi**, &c. (scc page 65), it should be treated as an independent item, because when such words are inflected, it is the base which changes and not the {gòdi}. It gives a generalizing sense to the base word, thus **sogòdi** "whatever, anything" (*cf.* **so** "what"), **kajgòdi** "wherever, everywhere" (*cf.* **kaj** "where"), and **kanagòdi** "whenever" (*cf.* **kàna** "when"). Some inflected forms include **sasagòdi** "with whatever," **savesagòdi** "with whichever" (masc.), **savjasagòdi** "with whichever" (fem.), **sostargòdi** "from whatever."

{-ìc-}   See {-ùc-}, below.

{-i-čh-}   A little-used diminutive suffix:

bakričho	"lamb"	(**o bakro** "sheep")
baličhi	"piglet"	(**o balo** "pig")

{-i-čòso}   This is the equivalent of *-ish* in English, *i.e.* it conveys some of the qualities of an adjective, but in a vague or unspecified way. The feminine singular subject has the same form as the masculine singular subject; the oblique masculine singular, and the oblique masculine and feminine plural, all take the suffix {-i-čosone} and the singular feminine oblique takes {-i-čosonja} (page 146):

bokhaličòso	"a bit hungry"	(e bokh "hunger")
kaličòso	"blackish"	(√kal- "black")
lindraličòso	"a bit sleepy"	(e lìndri "sleep")
loličòso	"reddish"	(√lol- "red")
nasvaličòso	"somewhat unwell"	(√nasval- "ill")
parničòso	"whitish, pale"	(√parn- "white")
rupuničòso	"a bit silvery"	(o rup "silver")
sumnakuničòso	"slightly golden"	(o sumnakaj "gold")

{-ìj-a}   This feminine nominal suffix, with stressed or unstressed /i/ conveys the idea of the entire domain of something. Its plural is with {-ìj-i}, and its oblique with {-ij-èn-}:

barvalikanìja	"world of the rich"	(√barval- "rich")
čorobìja	"wierdness"	(< čoròbo "wierd")
dragostìja	"love"	(√dràg- "beloved")
dušmanìja	"enmity, animosity"	(o dušman "enemy")
gadžikanìja	"non-Gypsy world"	(o gadžo "non-Gypsy")
gostìja	"hospitality"	(o gòsto "guest")
izelicìja	"treachery"	(< Slavic)
kurvìja	"harlotry"	(e kùrva "whore")
lojàcija	"loyalty"	(√lejàl- "loyal")
mundrìja	"beauty"	(√mùndr- "attractive")
rromanìja	"the Gypsy world"	(Rrom "Gypsy")
siguràncija	"safety, security"	(√sigùr- "safe, reliable")
špijonìja	"espionage"	(√špijòn- "spy")
tobolacìja	"auction"	(√tobol-i- "auction off")
xaranìja	"intelligentsia"	(√xaran- "intelligent")
veselìja	"happiness"	(√vesel- "happy")
vurrecìja	"hatred"	(√vurrìt- "disgusting")

The ending is applied to geographical and political domains, *i.e.* countries:

e **Ànglija**	"England"
e **Bèldžija**	"Belgium"
e **Erlàndija**	"Ireland"
e **Fràncija**	"France"
e **Grècija**	"Greece"
e **Makedònija**	"Macedonia"
e **Nòrija**	"Norway"
e **Norvègija**	"Norway"
e **Pharàtija**	"India"
e **Polònija**	"Poland"
e **Rumùnija**	"Romania"
e **Rrusìja**	"Russia"
e **Škipèrija**	"Albania"
e **Ulàndija**	"The Netherlands"
e **Ungàrija**	"Hungary"
e **Vizàntija**	"The Byzantine Empire"
e **Xorvàtija**	"Croatia"

It is also the equivalent of {*-ion*} in international vocabulary items:

asimilàcija	"assimilation"
integràcija	"integration"
ùnija	"union"
fùnkcija	"function"
nàcija	"nation," or "principal division of the Vlax"

{**-i-l-**}	This forms past participles from adjective-derived verbs (see also page 95):
	barilo "grown up" (√**bar-** "big")

{**-i-kan-**}	This is an adjectival suffix indicating human or human-like qualities. It increases the quality in

barikano	"proud, haughty"	(*cf.* **baro** "big"):
čhavorrikano	"childish, boyish"	(**o čhav(o)** "boy")
čorikano	"like a thief"	(**o čor** "thief")
devlikano	"godly, divine"	(**o d(ev)el** "god")
dilikano	"stupidly-behaving"	(**o dilo** "fool")
džuvlikano	"womanish, feminine"	(**e džuvli** "woman")

gadžikano	"non-Gypsilike"	(**o gadžo** "non-Gypsy")
manušikano	"human"	(**o manuš** "man")
mulikano	"deathly, deadly"	(**o mulo** "dead person")

{-(l)in}   This is a feminine nominal suffix of Armenian origin[1] which makes the name of the trcc or plant from the name of the fruit it bears:

akhorin	"nut tree"	(**o akhor** "(wal)nut")
ambrolin	"pear tree"	(**o ambrol** "pear")
aranxalin	"orange tree"	(**e arànxa** "orange")
dudulin	"pumpkin vine"	(**o dudum** "pumpkin")
khilavin	"plum tree"	(**e khilav** "plum")
ljubenicin	"melon vine"	(**e ljùbenica** "watermelon")
mesalinin	"olive tree"	(**e mesalìna** "olive")
persikalin	"peach tree"	(**e pèrsika** "peach")
phabajin	"apple tree"	(**e phabaj** "apple")
phabalin	"apple tree"	(**e phabaj** "apple")

Cf. Also

učhalin	"shadow"	< √**čhor-**	"spread over, cast, pour"
plajin	"hill"	< **plaj**	"mountain"
dopašin	"a half"	< **dopaš**	"half" (adj.)

{-n-}   In some words, this has an agentive function expressing "one who," "that which:"

bašno	"rooster"	(√**baš-** "make a noise")
čorno	"thief"	(√**čor-** "steal")
khosno	"napkin"	(√**khos-** "wipe")
piramno	"lover"	(√**pirj-** "copulate")
xoxamno	"liar"	(√**xoxav-** "lie")

Čorno, **piramno** and **xoxamno** also have the feminine forms **čorni** (see {-ni}), **piramni**, **xoxamni**.

{nà-}   See page 70.

{-ni}
{-in}   This is added to certain masculine animate nouns which end in a consonant, to create the feminine

---

[1]But *cf.* Sanskrit *hastin* "one possessing a hand" (i.e. "elephant") < *hasta* "hand."

equivalent, thus[1]:

čorni "female thief"(**o čor** "thief")
grasni "mare"   (**o grast** "horse")
gurumni "cow"   (**o guruv** "bull")
manušni "lady"   (**o manuš** "man")
ričhni "she-bear"   (**o rič**[2] "bear")
thagarni "queen"   (**o thagar**[2] "king")
But *cf.*
amalin   "female friend" (**o amal**[3] "friend")

{-**no**}   Used to make adjectives from international vocabulary items. such adjectives are athematic and are not changed for gender (see page 146).
politikàlno "political"
civìlno   "civil"

{-**òr-i**}   A masculine agentive suffix, a variant of {-**àr-i**}, above. This has the plural {-**òr-ja**}, the singular and plural oblique forms {-**or-è-s**} and {-**or-è-n**}, and the feminine {-**òr-ka**). The vocative for this is constructed with {-**òr-i-na**}.
khẹlitòri "dancer"   (√**khẹl**- "dance, play")
sitjaritòri "teacher"   (√**sitjar**- "teach, instruct")
pupujtòri "gossipmonger" (√**pupu-i**- "gossip")

{-**orr**-}   This adjectival suffix usually indicates a smaller size of something, *e.g.* **khẹrorro** "little house," or else to indicate that something is dear to one, *e.g.* **rromnjorri** "dear wife," even with adjectival roots: **loljorro** "nicely red." It can be used with numbers adjectivally to indicate precision (see page 168), **ačhilo de jekhorro minùto** "he waited for precisely

---

[1]Possibly related to this is the suffix {-**ri**} in **anguštri** "ring" (< **o anguš** "finger") and **menri** "necklace" (**e men** "neck") in other dialects (Vlax has **e angrusti** "ring," **o naj** "finger," **e korr** and **e men** "neck" and **o šìro** "necklace").
[2]The items are loans into some Vlax dialects from non-Vlax Romani.
[3]These words have become lost in American Vlax and have been replaced by **frenàki** (f.) and **frèno** (masc.), from English.

one minute," and likewise with other adjectives: **nevorro** "brand-new." It is used mainly with thematic roots, although not exclusively (see {-**ùc**-}, {-**ìc**-}); the athematic **mùca** "cat," and the thematic **bakro** "sheep," both have irregular diminutives with an intrusive /-š-/: **mucašorro, bakrišorro.**

{-**òs**-}   A little-used athematic suffix to form adjectives from nouns. The feminine subject singular has the same form as the masculine, all other forms have {-**o-n-e**} except for the feminine oblique singular, which has {-**o-n-ja**} (page 146):

milòso   "merciful, pitiful"   (**e mìla** "pity, mercy")
dragòso   "beloved"   (√**dràg**- "dear")
vurričòso   "hateful"   (√**vurrìt**- "disgusting")

{-**ùc**-}   This has a similar function to {-**orr**-}, above, but is mainly used with athematic roots: **Jankùco** "dear Yanko." *Cf.* also **korkorrùco** "poor lonely one" (< **kòrkorro** "alone"). The feminine is most commonly {-**ìc**-} as in **glabìca** "a small fine," although the masculine {-**ìc-o**} and the feminine {-**ùc-a**} are also very commonly used. It can also distinguish lexical meaning: **izvòno** "bell," **izvonùco** "a beep, tinkle;" **klàšto** "tongs," **klaštùco** "tweezers."

{-**un**-}   This has two distinct functions: first to describe the qualities of nouns, especially materials, as in **kaštuno** "wooden"(**o kašt** "wood"):

mortjuno   "leathern"   (**e mortji** "skin, leather")
phanrruno   "silken"   (**o phanrr** "silk")
sastruno   "iron, ferrous"   (**o sàstri** "iron")

Cf. Also

aratjuno   "yesterday's"   (**e rjat** "night" > **aratji** "yesterday:" **kado si aratjuno manrro** "this is yesterday['s] bread!")

The second function is to form adjectives from prepositions and prepositional adverbs:

angluno	"initial, first"	(àngla "before")
maškaruno	"intermediate"	(maškar "between")
opruno	"upper"	(opre "up")
paluno	"rear"	(pàla "behind")
pašuno	"adjacent, neighboring"	(pàša "near")
teluno	"lower"	(tèla "under")

{-ùtn-} This forms adjectives which relate to time or conditions. Some speakers treat this as an athematic suffix and keep the stress on the /-**u**-/, while others treat it as thematic, with thematic stress and morphology. Similary used athematic suffixes are {-**àln**-} and {-**èdn**-}.

(a)djesùtno	"today's"	(o djes "day")
akanutno	"contemporary, present-day"	(akana "now")
(a)ratjùtno	"tonight's"	(e rjat "night")
ivendùtno	"wintery"	(o ivend "winter")
khamùtno	"sunny"	(o kham "sun")
mirùtno	"peaceful"	(o mìro "peace, calm")
nilajùtno	"summery"	(e nilaj "summer")

Cf. Also

| šajùtno | "possible" | (šaj "able") |
| bišajùtno | "impossible" | (bi- + šaj "able") |

{-va}
{-vo} This is not a productive suffix, but one found in a small number of nouns with its origin in the Rumanian feminine singular termination {-**à**}, with euphonic /-**v**-/, and which has become an inseparable part of the Romani lexical root:

biròvo "office" (< *bureau*)
halavàva "halva"
kafàva "coffee;" also usu. **kàfa**
ljuljàva "tobacco pipe"
òblovo "circle, sphere"
pẹndjeràva"window;" also usu. **pẹndjèra, filjàstra**
vandrulòvo "hobo, tramp" (< Hung. *vándorol*)
vašalèvo "iron (for clothes)" (< Hung. *vasal*)
Žìdovo "Jew" (< Hung. *Zsidó*)

The Prefix {vàre-}

The prefix {vàre-} (or for some speakers of eastern Vlax {vèr-}) may be combined with various nominals and adverbials to give them a generalized sense:

kàna	"when"	vàrekana	"whenever, sometime"
kanagòdi	"whenever"	vàrekanagodi	"no matter when"
kaj	"where"	vàrekaj	"wherever, somewhere"
kajgòdi	"wherever"	vàrekajgodi	"anywhere else"
karing	"which way"	vàrekaring	"somewhere, someplace"
kasko	"whose"	vàrekasko	"someone's, whoever's"
kàtar	"where from"	vàrekatar	"from wherever"
kon	"who"	vàrekon	"whoever, someone"
sar	"how"	vàresar	"however, somehow"
sàvorre	"everyone"	vàresavorre	"whatever people"
savo	"which"	vàresavo	"any kind of"
so	"what"	vàreso	"something, anything"
sòde	"how much"	vàresode	"some, any; however much"
sòdja	"how many"	vàresodja	"some, any; however many"
sogòdi	"everything"	vàresogodi	"something, anything"
sòstar	"why"	vàresostar	"for some reason, for any reason"

Etymologies of the Verbal NFAs

Infixed verbal morphemes are either thematic or athematic. Those which are traceable to Sanskrit include:

1) {-er-} or {-ar-} (page 129, 130) in adjectival causative constructions, which is < √ker- "make, do." The full form is preserved in the Sinti dialects: **šilkerel** "he makes (s.t.) cold." The Central dialects have another verbal aspect constructed with √ker-, *viz.* the iterative, which is lacking in the Northern and Vlax dialects: **danderel** "he bites," **danderkerel** "he keeps on biting."

2) {-àv-} (pages 123, 124, 127, 128) is the verb √av-.

3) {-ov-} (pages 120, 125) is the verb √ov- "become." This has disappeared from Vlax, having fallen together with √av-. It survives in the Balkan dialects.

4) {-i-} (page 117) is from the Slavic infinitive stem.

5) {-**as**} (pages 84, 98) may be from the Sanskrit imperfective {**as**-}, or from Iranian {-**ast**} (Hancock, 1995:37-38).

6) {-**sar**-} (page 117) is compounded from underlying {-**as**-}, from Greek {-$\alpha\zeta\omega$}, plus the Gk. infinitive {-$\alpha\rho$-} (of Italic origin).

7) {-**ime**} (page 119) is the Greek middle passive participle {-$\mu\epsilon\nu o\varsigma$} (Sampson, §201).

8) {-**n**-} (pages 118, 119) is purely euphonic, according to Sampson (§263).

9) {-**l**-} (pages 90, 1222. 123. 126, 127) is the Sanskrit past participle {-*ta*} (Sampson, §195).

Nationalities and Languages

Nationalities

Names of members of national or ethnic groups usually have the singular endings {-**àn-o**}, masculine, and {-**àn-k-a**} or {-**àj-k-a**}, feminine, in the subject case, with the subject plurals {-**àj-a**} (m.) and {-**àn-k-i**}/{-**àn-č-i**} or {-**àj-k-i**}/{-**àj-č-i**} (f.) respectively. In the oblique case, these endings become {-**an-ò-s**}, {-**an-k-à**}/{-**aj-k-à**}, {-**ò-n**} and {-**an-k-è-n**}/{-**aj-k-è-n**}. The masculine singular vocative is with {-**ò-n-a**}, plural {-**è-j-a**}, feminine (singular only) takes {-**o**}:

Male		*Female*
Amerikàno	"American"	**Amerikànka** *or* **Amerikàjka**
Francuzàno	"French"	**Francuzànka** *or* **Francuzàjka**
Bečàno	"Viennese man"	**Bečànka** (< **Bèči** "Vienna")
Žịdovàno[1]	"Jew"	**Žịdovànka** *or* **Žịdovàjka**

Descriptors of nationalities are adjectival forms which have the following suffixes:

Masculine and feminine singular subject	{-**ìck-o**}
Masculine and feminine plural subject	{-**ìck-a**}
Masculine singular oblique	{-**ick-o-n-e**}
Feminine singular oblique	{-**ick-o-n-ja**}
Masculine and feminine plural oblique	{-**ì-ck-a**}

More often **Žịdovo** in American Vlax.

ekh francuzìcko **Rrom**	"a French Rom"
ekh mačvanìcko **Rromni**	"a Machvano woman"
duj amerikanìcka **gadže**	"two American non-Gypsies"
la mesikanickonja **dukatajkasa**	"with the Mexican female attorney"

Languages

Names of languages (*i.e.* as nouns) have only the {-ì-**ck-a**} form:

anglizìcka	"English"
djermanìcka	"German"
englišìcka	"English"
gadžikanìcka	"any language other than Romani"
kęldęrašìcka	"Kalderash"
lovarìcka	"Lovari"
mačvanìcka	"Machvano Romani" (Kalderash dialect)
mačvànska	"Machvano Romani" (Machvano dialect)
modjorìcka	"Hungarian"
njamcìcka	"German"
romaničelìcka	"Romanichal dialect"
rumunìcka	"Romanian"
rrusìcka	"Russian"
spanjolìcka	"Spanish"
škịperìcka	"Albanian"

Note also that language names can be expressed adverbially, *e.g.* **Rromanes** "Gypsily," *i.e.* in the Gypsy language, way, manner," &c. (see page 104).

Numerals

Cardinal Numbers: Subject

The first ten cardinal numbers in the subject case are

1 **jekh**   2 **duj**   3 **trin**   4 **štar**   5 **pandž**
6 **šov**   7 **efta**   8 **oxto**   9 **inja**   10 **deš**

From 11 to 19, (or in some dialects from 11 to 16), the numbers are compounded with {-u-}:

11 **deš-u-jekh**   12 **deš-u-duj**   13 **deš-u-trin**   14 **deš-u-štar**
15 **deš-u-pandž**   16 **deš-u-šov**
17 **deš-u-efta, deš-efta**
18 **deš-u-oxto, deš-oxto**
19 **deš-u-inja, deš-inja**

The multiples of ten up to 50 are

20 **biš**   30 **trànda**   40 **sarànda**   50 **pìnda**

Above this, they are compounded using unstressed {-var(-)} "times," which forms are also possible for 30, 40 and 50 (and more commonly their forms in American Vlax):
30 **tri-var-deš** (written **trivardeš**)
40 **štarvardeš**
50 **pandžvardeš**
60 **šovardeš**
70 **eftavardeš**
80 **oxtovardeš**
90 **injavardeš**

Some speakers include in their speech the following alternative forms based on multiples of twenty:
40 **duvarbiš**
60 **trivarbiš**
80 **štarvarbiš**

Note the forms **dùvar** "twice" (not *__dùjvar__) and **trìvar** "thrice" (and not *__trìnvar__). {-var(-)} occurs in the compound forms **vùnivar** "sometimes," **butìvar** (or **bùtvar**) "often" and **sòdevar** "how often?."
Combinations of multiples of tens with units are compounded with **ta**:
21 **biš-ta-jekh**
22 **biš-ta-duj**
44 **štarvàrdeš-ta-štar**

53 **pìnda-ta-trin**
53 **pandžvàrdeš-ta-trin**
64 **šovàrdeš-ta-štar**
85 **oxtovàrdeš-ta-pandž**
99 **injavàrdeš-ta-inja**

"One hundred," 100, is **jekh šel**, 200 is **duj šela** and so on, although hundreds and higher numbers are not pluralized in their ordinal forms.

"One thousand," 1,000, is **jekh mìja**, 2,000 is **duj mìji**, and so on. In Hungarian Lovari, "thousand" is **èzer**, pl. **ezèra** (< Hung.).

"One million," 1,000,000, is **jekh miljòno**, 2,000,000 is **duj miljòja**, although the alternative plural forms **miljònurja** and **miljòni** also occur.

The word for "zero" is **nul** or **nùla** in eastern European Vlax, but **zìro**, **kòlo** (*lit.* "circle") or **rr(o)àta** (*lit.* "wheel") in American Vlax.

The word for "a dozen" is **ekh djùžena**.

There is a special number used in counting money in lots of fifty dollars: **lìra**.

pandž lìri   "two hundred and fifty dollars"
biš lìri   "a thousand dollars"

note also the work **frànka** (plural **frànki**, **frànči**) used for twenty-five cents:

potjindem trin frànči pe leste "I paid 75¢ for it"

Cardinal Numbers: Oblique

In the oblique case, the numbers from one to ten when they are functioning adjectivally have the following forms:
1 **jekhe** (m.) or **jekha** (f.),   2 **do**,   3 **trine**,   4 **štare**,   5 **pandže**,
   6 **šove**, (7-9 are the same as the subject case),   10 **deše**

When these are nouns, they take the expected nominal suffixes. The numeral "two" has the nominal root {√**don(-)**}:
dikhlem jekhes   "I saw one" (*e.g.* one person)
džava me le donenca "I'm going with the two (of them)"

Ordinal Numbers

These are made with the Greek-derived unstressed suffix {-t-o}. Multiples of numbers are not pluralized when ordinal (**trin šèlto** "three hundredth," *not *trin šelàto*):

1st	**jèkhto**
2nd	**dùjto**
3rd	**trìto** (*not *trìnto*)
4th	**štàrto**
5th	**pàndžto**
6th	**šòvto**
10th	**dèšto**
20th	**bìšto**
30th	**tràndato**
67th	**šovardeš-ta-enjàto**
99th	**injavardeš-ta-injàto**
888th	**oxto šela oxtovardeš-ta-oxtòto**

The ordinal suffix can be added to **sòde** "how much" to give **sodèto** "the what, what number" in the context of a number or position in a sequence: **Sodèto san tume akana?** "What number are you now?" (to people waiting in line); **sodèto si adjes** "the what (of the month) is it today?."

In the oblique case, the endings are the regular athematic adjectival suffixes {-on-e}, {-on-j-a}.

"First" may be translated in a number of ways: **jèkhto**, **angluno** and (athematic) **pèrvo**, although only **jèkhto** can be used with ordinal numbers over ten. As an adverb, "firstly" is **anglunes**, **pervones** or just **pèrvo**.

"Last" as an adjective is **palèdno, palùtno** or **paluno**, though the word is not often used. "Lastly" as an adverb is **agore, agoreste**, **'goreste** or **and'e vùrma**. "Later on" or "after" is **maj palal** (or **maj pòšle** in Machvano Vlax).

Fractions include **o** (or for some speakers **e**) **dopašin** "half" (but **dopaš** as an adjective, and **paš-dopaš** "half and half;" *cf.* also √**dopaš-i-** "to divide in two"), and **o futàri** or **furtàri** "quarter."

Other fractions are made using ordinal numbers, thus **duj trìturja** "two thirds," **trin pàndžturja** "three fifths," &c.

Other Numerical Forms

Written numbers have names, just as letters of the alphabet have names in English. In Romani, these are made by suffixing {-alì} to the cardinal root: **jekhali** "number one," **dujali** "number two," **bišali** "number twenty," **šelali** "number one hundred."

The independent stressed word **lì** is a kind of definite article restricted to use with numerals. It gives the idea of the whole group of that number: **lì-trin** "all three," **lì-deš** "all ten," **malad-ilem sa li-trinèn** "I met all three of them." **Lì-duj** can be used to translate "both," but commoner expressions for this are **sa'l duj, so'l duj** or **vi'l duj**. note also **pe lì-štar** "on all fours."

Some speakers have a separate inflected form **sàre** for the oblique case of **sa** "all:" **maladilem sare li-trinen**.

Po is used when distributing numbers of items: **po duj** "by twos," **po trin** "by threes," **thodja len po-efta** "he set them out in groups of seven." *Cf.* also **po cìrra** "little by little."

Po or **de** together with an ordinal numeral root plus the suffix {-ùle} (that is, -t-ùle}) expresses sequences of times: **po dujtùle** "for the second time," **de tritùle ansurime sas** "he got married for the third time," &c. A variant pronunciation of {-ùle} is {-òlja}.

The diminutive {-orr-} with cardinal numbers expresses the idea of precision: **dujorre džene** "exactly two people," **oxtorre teljàrja** "exactly eight dollars," **ka'l jekhorro** "at precisely one (o'clock)."

With numbers above one, the plural genitive prepositional ending is used with people's ages, as well as when referring to numbers on playing cards. The same affixes are applied to **sòde** "how much," to mean "how old?:" **Sodengi la? Biš-ta-dongi** "How old is she? Twenty two;" **Sodengo lo? Trànda-ta-štarengo** "How old is he? Thirty four." Note also **but** "many, much," oblique **bute, xanci** "not many, not much," and **ekh cìrra** or **ekh falàto** "a little ~."

but džene   "many people" (pronounced **bu' džene**)

bute dženenca	"with many people"
xanci džene	"few people"
'kh cìrra mol	"a little wine"
ekh falàto kirjal	"a little cheese"

Telling Time

Ways of telling the time in American Vlax differ slightly from European Vlax.

Hours are plural, even one o'clock, and are used with **ka le (ka'l)**, with or without **čàsurja** "hours" when expressing "to ~:" **ka'l jekh** or **ka'l jekh čàso** "at one o'clock," **ka'l efta** "at seven," &c.

In European Vlax, numbers of minutes *past* the hour are indicated with **thaj/aj** "and:" **deš thaj biš** "twenty minutes past ten," **pandž aj dopaš** "five thirty," **štar aj furtàri** "a quarter past four." In American Vlax, **pàla** "after" is used instead of **thaj**: **deš pàla efta** "ten after seven."

In European Vlax, numbers of minutes *to* the hour are expressed as the next hour less the number of minutes, thus **deš-u-duj bi-furtarèsko** "a quarter to twelve," **trin bi-štarengo** "four minutes to three, " **ka'l duj bi-bišengo** "at twenty to two." In American Vlax, **ka** is used instead: **štar ka'l deš-u-duj** "four minutes to twelve," **jekh furtàri ka'l trin** "a quarter to three," **ka'l biš minùtji ka'l duj** "at twenty minutes to two."

Words associated with periods of time are given on page 106; names of the days of the week are listed on pages 106 and 107. Some other related vocabulary includes:

adjes	"today"
djes-djesestar	from day to day, day by day"
aratji	"yesterday"
aver-aratji	"the day before yesterday"
aratjuno	"yesterday's" *adj.*
aver-iš	"the day before yesterday"
berš[1]	"year"
o berš k'avel	"next year"

---

[1]The word **berš** often follows the year and is hyphenated to it ("**1945-berš**"), especially in publications from eastern Europe.

o berš nakhlo	"last year"
o kaver berš	"next year; last year"
kol berš	"some years back"
čhon[1]	"month"
kol čhonendar	"some months ago"
de dimnjàca	"morning"
kurko	"week"
kol kurkendar	"some weeks ago"
mizmèri	"noon"
pàla-mizmèri	"afternoon"
mjazùco	"noon"
pàla-mjazùco	"afternoon"
pèrsi	"last year"[2]
rjat	"night"
de kuratjàra	"since the day before yesterday"
de ratjàko	"in the evening"
tehàra	"tomorrow"
aver-tehàra	"the day after tomorrow"
over-tehàra	"the day after tom,orrow"

There are no universally used month names. Either the names in the language of the country are used, conforming to Romani grammar or not, or else they are numbered: **pèrvo čhon** "January," **dujto čhon** "February," **trito čhon** "March," &c. The new international standard uses a similar number-based system, employing the unstressed suffix {**-naj**}: **pèrvonaj, dùjtonaj, trìtonaj, štàrtonaj,** &c.

---

[1]The original word for "month," **masak**, has been lost in Vlax and replaced by **čhon** "moon." Since "moon" now means "month," the word for "moonlight," **čhonùto**, has now come to mean "moon;" this is a thematic item which behaves athematically because of its stress placement. "Moonlight" is **čhonutoski vedjàrja**.
[2]This is found only in western Vlax dialects and is of Greek origin (< πέρυσι); the same dialects have **popèrsi** "two years ago."

A Note on the Use of Core forms

Core forms are those words and expressions which belong to the oldest strata of the language, as opposed to accreted, or adopted, lexical and idiomatic material from the later periods. It is natural that, for Romani-speaking populations which have lived for a long time in another linguistic territory, for example Romanian Vlax Roma who have lived for hundreds of years among the Romanians, or American Roma who have lived for a century among English speakers, words and expressions from those non-Gypsy languages should make an impact upon Romani. But as the Romani-speaking populations throughout the world begin to communicate with each other, it has quickly become evident that, while "core" vocabulary is everywhere understood, newly adopted words and calques (that is, translations of non-Romani idioms into Romani) cause problems of communication.

Very often, the core form of a word or expression still exists alongside its newer adopted equivalent and, especially in international communication, an effort should be made to use these. The fewer non-Romani words one uses in one's speech, the better and more widely will it be understood. These include metaphorical usages, which are also widely understood, such as **drakhin** for "network" (*lit.* "grapevine") or **čhiriklo** "aeroplane" (*lit.* "bird"). Some of adopted forms where core forms could be used instead, include:

	Non-Core Forms	*Alternative Core forms*
"he begins"	**kẹzdil, načinajil**	**thol pe te, lel pe te**
"he feels like"	**bẹnuil te**	**avel les te**
"he has to"	**mùsaj leske te**	**si te, si leske te**
"he translates"	**tolmačil**	**parruvel**
"he speaks fluently"	**del dùma tẹkučones**	**vrakerel sar o paj**
"how do you say ~?"	**sar tolmačis ~?**	**sar phenel-pe ~?**
"what's happening?"	**so slučajil?**	**so džal-pe? so nakhel?**
"always"	**sàgda**	**sarevar, sar'var**
"difference"	**difẹrèncija**	**averutnipe**

"in every land"	**ande sàko them**	**ande sosko them**
"for" (a length of time)	**de**	**pe**
"how (big, nice, &c.)!"	**če ~!**	**so'i ~!**
"lungs"	**plumùni**	**parne buke**[1]
"marginal"	**vurmàko**	**agoruno, riguno**
"moment"	**momènt**	**jekhatar**
"my own house"	**m'o vlàsno kher**	**m'o čačuno kher**
"never"	**šòha**	**nìvar, nàvar, čìvar**
"not even"	**či dàži**	**či na či**
"older"	**maj phuro**	**phureder**
"ordinary"	**pròsto**	**savorrengo**
"still"	**ìnkę, još**	**sa**
"suddenly"	**tistàra, izdràzo**	**sa (de) jekh**
"the same place"	**o ìsto than, o mìzmo than**	**sa godo than**
"union"	**ùnija, kòlo**	**phandipe**
"what kind of"	**če fjàlo**	**savestar, sosko**
"wrist"	**ankitùra**	**vasteski phurt**

---

[1]This is assumed by many Romani speakers to be a "native" idiom, but is in fact a Slavic-derived calque, *cf.* Bulgarian бял дроб, *lit.* "white liver," (and черен дроб "liver," *lit.* "black liver" in the same language).

Works Mentioned in the Text

Bhattacharya, Deben, 1965. *The Gypsies.* London: Record Books.
Berger, H., 1969. "Die Burušaski-Lehnwörter in der Zigeunersprache," *Indo-Iranian Journal,* 3(1):17-43.
Boltz, William, & Michael Shapiro (eds.), 1990. *Studies in the Historical Phonology of Asian Languages.* Philadelphia & Amsterdam: John Benjamins.
Brockhaus, *in* Pott, Volume I, *p.* 42.
Chatard, J. & M. Bernard, 1959. *Zanko: Chef Tribal.* Paris: La Colombe.
Chauhan, R.R.S., 1994. *Africans in India: From Slavery to Royalty.* New Delhi: Asian Publications Services.
Cortiade, Marcel, 1988. *Morfologija e gjuhës rrome të përbashkët.* Titograd & Prishtinë: Peskekerdo.
Cortiade, Marcel, 1994. *Phonologie des Parlers Rom et Diasystème Graphique de la Langue Romani.* Doctoral thesis, University of the Sorbonne.
De Goeje, M.J., 1875. *Mémoire sur les Migrations des Tsiganes à Travers l'Asie.* Mémoires d'Histoire et de Géographie Orientales No. 3, Leiden: Brill.
Doerfer, Gerhard, 1970. "Irano-Altaistica: Turkish and Mongolian languages of Persia and Afghanistan," *in* Sebeok, 1970, *pp.* 217-234.
Grierson, George A., 1922. *Linguistic Survey of India.* Delhi: Motilal Banarsidass.
Hancock, Ian, 1995. "On the migration and affiliation of the Ḍōmba: Iranian words in Rom, Lom and Dom Gypsy," *in* Matras, 1995, *pp.* 29-59.
Hancock, Ian, 1993. "The Hungarian student Istvan Vályi and the Indian connection of Romani," *Lacio Drom,* 44:17-23.
Hancock, Ian, 1990. "Vlax phonological divergence from Common Romani," *in* Boltz & Shapiro, 1990, *pp.* 54-65.
Hancock, Ian, 1988. "The development of Romani linguistics," *in* Jazyery & Winter, 1988, *pp.* 183-223.
Hancock, Ian, 1984. "Romani and Angloromani," *in* Trudgill, 1984, *pp.* 367-383.

174

Hancock, Ian, (ed.), 1979. *Romani Sociolinguistics* [= *International Journal of the Sociology of Language*], Vol. 19.

Hill, 1993. *¿Kaj si o Rukun Amaro?*. London: Ventura Ltd.

Hill, 1994. *O Rukun ʒal and-i Skòla*. London: Ventura Ltd.

Hill, 1995. *I Bari Lavenqi Pustik e Rukunesqiri*. London: Ventura.

Ibbetson, Denzil C.J., 1881. *Census Report for the Punjab*. Calcutta: India Foreign Office.

Jazyery, Ali, & Werner Winter (eds.), 1988. *Languages and Cultures: Studies in Honor of Edgar C. Polomé*. Berlin & New York: Mouton de Gruyter.

Joshi, A., 1981. "Romani as a mediaeval Aryan language," *Roma*, 6(1):37-39.

Jusuf, S., & Krume Kepeski, 1980. *Romani Gramatika - Romska Gramatika*. Skopje: Naša Kniga.

Kaufman, Terrence, 1979. "Review of W.R. Rishi's *Multilingual Romani Dictionary*," in Hancock, 1979, *pp.* 131-144.

Kaufman, Terrence, 1984. "Explorations in Proto-Gypsy phonology and classification," Paper read at the Sixth South Asian Languages Analysis Round Table, Austin, May 25th-26th.

Kenrick, Donald, 1994. *Les Tsiganes de l'Inde à la Méditerranée*. Toulouse: Collection Interface, Centre de Recherches Tsiganes.

Kochanowski, Vania de Gila, 1968. "Black Gypsies, white Gypsies," *Diogenes*, 63:27-47.

Lal, Chaman, 1962. *Gypsies: Forgotten Children of India*. Delhi: Ministry of Information and Broadcasting.

Lorimer, D.L.R., 1937. "Burushaski and its alien neighbours: Problems in linguistic contagion," *Transactions of the Philological Society*, 1937:63-98.

Matras, Yaron (ed.), 1995. *Romani in Contact: The History, Sociology and Structure of a Language*. Amsterdam: John Benjamins.

Minturn, Leigh, & John T. Hitchcock, 1966. *The Rājpūts of Khalapur, India*. New York & London: John Wiley & Sons.

Paspati, Alexandre G., 1870. *Etude sur les Tchinghianés ou Bohémiens de l'Empire Ottoman*. Constantinople: Karoméla.

Piasere, Leonardo, 1988. "De origine Cinganorum," in Stahl, 1988, *pp.* 105-126.

Pischel, Richard, 1883. "Die Heimath der Zigeuner," *Deutsche Rundschau*, 36:353-375.

Pott, August, 1844. *Die Zigeuner in Europea und Asien.* Halle: Heynemann Verlag.

Rajshekar, V.T., 1987. *Dalit: The Black Untouchables of India.* Atlanta & Ottawa: Clarity Press.

Rishi, Weer R., 1975. *Roma: The Punjabi Emigrants in Europe, Central and Middle Asia, the USSR and the Americas.* Patiala: Punjabi Press.

Redžosko, Yanko le, 1984. "Armenian contributions to the Gypsy language," *Ararat*, 25(4):2-6.

Sarău, Gheorghe, 1992. *Mic Dicţionar Rom-Român.* Bucharest: Kriterion.

Sarău, Gheorghe, 1994. *Limba Romani: Manual pentru Clasele de Invăţători Romi ale Şcolilor Normale.* Bucharest: Editura Didactică şi Pedagogică.

Sebeok, Thomas (ed.), 1970. *Current Trends in Linguistics 6: Linguistics in South West Asia and North Africa.* The Hague: Mouton.

Shashi, S.S., 1990. *Roma: The Gypsy World.* Delhi: Sandeep Prakashan.

Singal, D.P., 1982. *Gypsies: Indians in Exile.* Meerut: Archana Publications.

Stahl, P.H. (ed.), 1988. *Recueil.* Paris: Etudes et Documents Balkaniques et Méditerranéens.

Stojka, Mongo, 1994. *Amari Luma.* Vienna: Gypsy-Production. CD liner notes and song texts.

Sutherland, Anne, 1975. *Gypsies: The Hidden Americans.* London: Macmillan.

Thomas, J.D. *et al.*, 1987. "Disease, lifestyle and consanguinity in 58 American Gypsies," *The Lancet*, August 25th, *pp.* 377-379.

Trudgill, Peter (ed.), 1984. *Languages in the British Isles.* Cambridge: The University Press.

Watson, Francis, 1988. *A Concise History of India.* London: Thames & Hudson.

Willems, Wim, 1995. *Op Zoek naar de Ware Zigeuner: Zigeuners als Studieobject Tijdens de Verlichting, de Romantiek en het Nazisme.* Utrecht: Uitgeverij Jan van Arkel.

176

Index

FOR NOTES

FOR NOTES

Other Books From Slavica

Ronelle Alexander: *The Structure of Vasko Popa's Poetry.*

American Contributions to the Eleventh International Congress of Slavists (Bratislava, 1993), Literature, Linguistics, Poetics, ed. Robert A. Maguire and Alan Timberlake.

American Contributions to the Tenth International Congress of Slavists, Sofia, September, 1988, Linguistics, ed. Alexander M. Schenker.

American Contributions to the Tenth International Congress of Slavists, Sofia, September, 1988, Literature, ed. Jane Gary Harris.

American Contributions to the Ninth International Congress of Slavists (Kiev 1983) Vol. 1: Linguistics, ed. Michael S. Flier.

American Contributions to the Ninth International Congress of Slavists, (Kiev 1983) Vol. 2: Literature, Poetics, History, ed. P. Debreczeny.

American Contributions to the Eighth International Congress of Slavists, Vol 1: Linguistics and Poetics, ed. Henrik Birnbaum.

American Contributions to the Eighth International Congress of Slavists Vol. 2: Literature, ed. Victor Terras.

Patricia M. Arant: *Russian for Reading.*

James Daniel Armstrong in memoriam.

Howard I. Aronson: *Georgian: A Reading Grammar.*

Howard I. Aronson, ed.: *Non-Slavic Languages of the USSR Papers from the Fourth Conference.*

Bayara Aroutunova: *Lives in Letters Princess Zinaida Volkonskaya and Her Correspondence.*

James Bailey: *Three Russian Lyric Folk Song Meters.*

Natalya Baranskaya: *Неделя как неделя Just Another Week*, ed. *Lora Paperno, Natalie Roklina*, and *Richard Leed.*

Adele Marie Barker: *The Mother Syndrome in the Russian Folk Imagination.*

R. P. Bartlett, A. G. Cross, and Karen Rasmussen, eds.: *Russia and the World of the Eighteenth Century.*

Other Books From Slavica

John D. Basil: *The Mensheviks in the Revolution of 1917.*

Christina Y. Bethin: *Polish Syllables   The Role of Prosody in Phonology and Morphology.*

Henrik Birnbaum & Thomas Eekman, eds.: *Fiction and Drama in Eastern and Southeastern Europe: Evolution and Experiment in the Postwar Period.*

Henrik Birnbaum and Peter T. Merrill: *Recent Advances in the Reconstruction of Common Slavic (1971-1982).*

Marianna D. Birnbaum: *Humanists in a Shattered World: Croatian and Hungarian Latinity in the Sixteenth Century.*

F. J. Bister and Herbert Kuhner, eds.: *Carinthian Slovenian Poetry.*

K. L. Black, ed.: *A Biobibliographical Handbook of Bulgarian Authors.*

Ralph Bogert: *The Writer as Naysayer   Miroslav Krleža and the Aesthetic of Interwar Central Europe.*

Marianna Bogojavlensky: *Russian Review Grammar.*

Rodica C. Botoman, Donald E. Corbin, E. Garrison Walters: *Îmi Place Limba Română/A Romanian Reader.*

Richard D. Brecht and James S. Levine, eds: *Case in Slavic.*

Gary L. Browning: *Workbook to <u>Russian Root List</u>.*

Ranko Bugarski and Celia Hawkesworth, eds.: *Language Planning in Yugoslavia.*

Diana L. Burgin: *Richard Burgin   A Life in Verse.*

R. L. Busch: *Humor in the Major Novels of Dostoevsky.*

Terence R. Carlton: *Introduction to the Phonological History of the Slavic Languages.*

Catherine V. Chvany and R. D. Brecht, eds.: *Morphosyntax in Slavic.*

Jozef Cíger-Hronský: *Jozef Mak* (a novel), translated from Slovak.

Julian W. Connolly & Sonia I. Ketchian, eds.: *Studies in Honor of Vsevolod Setchkarev.*

Other Books From Slavica

Henry R. Cooper, Jr. ed.: *Papers in Slovene Studies 1978.*

Andrew R. Corin: *The New York Missal: A Paleographic and Phonetic Analysis.*

Gary Cox: *Tyrant and Victim in Dostoevsky.*

Anna Lisa Crone and Catherine V. Chvany, eds.: *New Studies in Russian Language and Literature.*

Paul Cubberley: *Handbook of Russian Affixes.*

Carolina De Maegd-Soëp: *Chekhov and Women: Women in the Life and Work of Chekhov.*

William W. Derbyshire: *A Basic Reference Grammar of Slovene.*

Stefana Dimitrova: *Исключения в русском языке*

Dorothy Disterheft: *The Syntactic Development of the Infinitive in Indo-European.*

Per Durst-Andersen: *Mental Grammar Russian Aspect and Related Issues.*

Thomas Eekman and Dean S. Worth, eds.: *Russian Poetics.*

M. J. Elson: *Macedonian Verbal Morphology A Structural Analysis.*

M. S. Flier and R. D. Brecht, eds.: *Issues in Russian Morphosyntax.*

M. S. Flier and A. Timberlake, eds: *The Scope of Slavic Aspect.*

John M. Foley, ed.: *Oral Traditional Literature A Festschrift for Albert Bates Lord.*

John Miles Foley, ed.: *Comparative Research on Oral Traditions: A Memorial for Milman Parry.*

Richard Frucht, ed.: *Labyrinth of Nationalism, Complexities of Diplomacy Essays in Honor of Charles and Barbara Jelavich.*

Isidore Geld: *Dictionary of Omissions for Russian Translators with Examples from Scientific Texts*

Zbigniew Gołąb: *The Origin of the Slavs A Linguist's View.*

Gerald Greenberg: *Beginning Russian Computer Exercises for DOS.*

Other Books From Slavica

Diana Greene: *Insidious Intent: An Interpretation of Fedor Sologub's The Petty Demon*.

Charles E. Gribble, ed.: *Medieval Slavic Texts, Vol. 1, Old and Middle Russian Texts*.

Charles E. Gribble: *Reading Bulgarian Through Russian*.

Charles E. Gribble: *Russian Root List with a Sketch of Word Formation*.

Charles E. Gribble: *A Short Dictionary of 18th-Century Russian/ Словарик Русского Языка 18-го Века*.

Charles E. Gribble, ed.: *Studies Presented to Professor Roman Jakobson by His Students*.

George J. Gutsche and Lauren G. Leighton, eds.: *New Perspectives on Nineteenth-Century Russian Prose*.

Morris Halle, ed.: *Roman Jakobson: What He Taught Us*.

Morris Halle, Krystyna Pomorska, Elena Semeka-Pankratov, and Boris Uspenskij, eds.: *Semiotics and the History of Culture In Honor of Jurij Lotman Studies in Russian*.

Charles J. Halperin: *The Tatar Yoke*.

William S. Hamilton: *Introduction to Russian Phonology and Word Structure*.

Pierre R. Hart: *G. R. Derzhavin: A Poet's Progress*.

Michael Heim: *Contemporary Czech*.

Michael Heim, Z. Meyerstein, and Dean Worth: *Readings in Czech*.

Warren H. Held, Jr., William R. Schmalstieg, and Janet E. Gertz: *Beginning Hittite*.

Peter Hill: *The Dialect of Gorno Kalenik*.

M. Hubenova & others: *A Course in Modern Bulgarian*.

Martin E. Huld: *Basic Albanian Etymologies*.

Charles Isenberg: *Substantial Proofs of Being: Osip Mandelstam's Literary Prose*.

Roman Jakobson: *Brain and Language*

Other Books From Slavica

L. A. Johnson: *The Experience of Time in* <u>Crime and Punishment</u>.

S. J. Kirschbaum, ed.: *East European History (Selected Papers from the Third World Congress for Soviet and East European Studies)*.

Emily R. Klenin: *Animacy in Russian: A New Interpretation*.

Andrej Kodjak, Krystyna Pomorska, and Kiril Taranovsky, eds.: *Alexander Puškin Symposium II*.

Andrej Kodjak, Krystyna Pomorska, Stephen Rudy, eds.: *Myth in Literature*.

Andrej Kodjak: *Pushkin's I. P. Belkin*.

Andrej Kodjak, Michael J. Connolly, Krystyna Pomorska, eds.: *Structural Analysis of Narrative Texts*.

Demetrius J. Koubourlis, ed.: *Topics in Slavic Phonology*.

Mark Kulikowski: *A Bibliography of Slavic Mythology*.

Konstantin Kustanovich: *The Artist and the Tyrant: Vassily Aksenov's Works in the Brezhnev Era*.

Ronald D. LeBlanc: *The Russianization of Gil Blas: A Study in Literary Appropriation*.

Richard L. Leed, Alexander D. Nakhimovsky, and Alice S. Nakhimovsky: *Beginning Russian, Second Revised Edition*.

Richard L. Leed and Slava Paperno: *5000 Russian Words With All Their Inflected Forms: A Russian-English Dictionary*.

Edgar H. Lehrman: *A Handbook to Eighty-Six of Chekhov's Stories in Russian*.

Lauren Leighton, ed.: *Studies in Honor of Xenia Gąsiorowska*.

Gail Lenhoff: *The Martyred Princes Boris and Gleb: A Social-Cultural Study of the Cult and the Texts*.

Jules F. Levin and Peter D. Haikalis, with Anatole A. Forostenko: *Reading Modern Russian*.

Maurice I. Levin: *Russian Declension and Conjugation: A Structural Description with Exercises*.

Alexander Lipson: *A Russian Course*.

Other Books From Slavica

Alexander Lipson in Memoriam.

Yvonne R. Lockwood: *Text and Context Folksong in a Bosnian Muslim Village.*

A Sense of Place Tsarskoe Selo and Its Poets Papers from the 1989 Dartmouth Conference Dedicated to the Centennial of Anna Akhmatova, ed. Lev Loseff and Barry Scherr.

Sophia Lubensky and Donald K. Jarvis, eds.: *Teaching, Learning, Acquiring Russian.*

Horace G. Lunt: *Fundamentals of Russian.*

Paul Macura: *Russian-English Botanical Dictionary.*

Thomas G. Magner, ed.: *Slavic Linguistics and Language Teaching.*

Robert Mann: *Lances Sing: A Study of the Igor Tale.*

Stephen Marder: *A Supplementary Russian-English Dictionary.*

V. Markov and D. S. Worth, eds.: *From Los Angeles to Kiev Papers on the Occasion of the Ninth International Congress of Slavists.*

Cynthia L. Martin, Joanna Robin, and Donald K. Jarvis: *The Russian Desk: A Listening and Conversation Course.*

Mateja Matejić and Dragan Milivojević: *An Anthology of Medieval Serbian Literature in English.*

Peter J. Mayo: *The Morphology of Aspect in Seventeenth-Century Russian (Based on Texts of the Smutnoe Vremja).*

Arnold McMillin, ed.: *Aspects of Modern Russian and Czech Literature (Selected Papers from the Third World Congress for Soviet and East European Studies).*

Gordon M. Messing: *A Glossary of Greek Romany As Spoken in Agia Varvara (Athens).*

Vasa D. Mihailovich and Mateja Matejic: *A Comprehensive Bibliography of Yugoslav Literature in English, 1593-1980.*

Vasa D. Mihailovich: *First Supplement to* A Comprehensive Bibliography of Yugoslav Literature in English *1981-1985.*

Vasa D. Mihailovich: *Second Supplement to* A Comprehensive Bibliography of Yugoslav Literature in English *1981-1985.*

Other Books From Slavica

Michael J. Mikoś, ed. & trans.: *Polish Renaissance Literature   An Anthology.*

Dragan Milivojević and Vasa D. Mihailovich: *A Bibliography of Yugoslav Linguistics in English   1900-1980.*

Edward Możejko, ed.: *Vasiliy Pavlovich Aksënov: A Writer in Quest of Himself.*

Edward Możejko: *Yordan Yovkov.*

Alexander D. Nakhimovsky and Richard L. Leed: *Advanced Russian, Second Edition, Revised.*

The Comprehensive Russian Grammar of A. A. Barsov/Обстоятельная грамматика А. А. Барсова, Critical Edition by Lawrence W. Newman.

Wiesław Oleksy and Oscar E. Swan: *W Labiryncie (Labyrinth of Life) opera mydlana w dwudziestu jeden odcinkach oparta na motywach serialu telewizyjnego w reżyserii Pawła Karpińskiego* (a video-based advanced Polish language course).

Hongor Oulanoff: *The Prose Fiction of Veniamin Kaverin.*

T. Pachmuss: *Russian Literature in the Baltic between the World Wars.*

Lora Paperno: *Getting Around Town in Russian: Situational Dialogs*, English translation and photographs by Richard D. Sylvester.

Slava Paperno, Alexander D. Nakhimovsky, Alice S. Nakhimovsky, and Richard L. Leed: *Intermediate Russian: The Twelve Chairs.*

Ruth L. Pearce: *Russian For Expository Prose.*

Jan L. Perkowski: *The Darkling   A Treatise on Slavic Vampirism.*

Gerald Pirog: *Aleksandr Blok's Итальянские Стихи   Confrontation and Disillusionment.*

Leonard A. Polakiewicz: *Supplemental Materials for First Year Polish.*

Stanley J. Rabinowitz: *Sologub's Literary Children: Keys to a Symbolist's Prose.*

Other Books From Slavica

Gilbert C. Rappaport: *Grammatical Function and Syntactic Structure: The Adverbial Participle of Russian.*

David F. Robinson: *Lithuanian Reverse Dictionary.*

Klaus Roth and Gabriele Wolf: *South Slavic Folk Culture A Bibliography.*

Don Karl Rowney, ed.: *Imperial Power and Development: Papers on Pre-Revolutionary Russian History (Selected Papers from the Third World Congress for Soviet and East European Studies).*

Don K. Rowney & G. Edward Orchard, eds.: *Russian and Slavic History.*

Klaus Roth and Gabriele Wolf, eds.: *South Slavic Folk Culture A Bibliography.*

Catherine Rudin: *Aspects of Bulgarian Syntax: Complementizers and WH Constructions.*

Norma L. Rudinsky: *Incipient Feminists: Women Writers in the Slovak National Revival.*

Gerald J. Sabo, S.J., ed.: *Valaská Škola, by Hugolin Gavlovič*, with a linguistic sketch by Ľubomír Ďurovič.

Barry P. Scherr and Dean S. Worth, eds.: *Russian Verse Theory.*

William R. Schmalstieg: *Introduction to Old Church Slavic.*

William R. Schmalstieg: *A Lithuanian Historical Syntax.*

R. D. Schupbach: *Lexical Specialization in Russian.*

Elena Semeka-Pankratov, ed.: *Studies in Poetics Commemorative Volume Krystyna Pomorska (1928-1986).*

P. Seyffert: *Soviet Literary Structuralism: Background Debate Issues.*

Kot K. Shangriladze and Erica W. Townsend, eds: *Papers for the V. Congress of Southeast European Studies (Belgrade, September 1984).*

J. Thomas Shaw: *Pushkin A Concordance to the Poetry.*

J. Thomas Shaw: *Pushkin's Poetry of the Unexpected: The Non-rhymed Lines in the Rhymed Poetry, and The Rhymed Lines in the Nonrhymed Poetry.*

Other Books From Slavica

Efraim Sicher: *Style and Structure in the Prose of Isaak Babel'*.

Rimvydas Šilbajoris: *Tolstoy's Aesthetics and His Art*.

M. S. Simpson: *The Russian Gothic Novel and its British Antecedents*.

David A. Sloane: *Aleksandr Blok and the Dynamics of the Lyric Cycle*.

Greta N. Slobin, ed.: *Aleksej Remizov: Approaches to a Protean Writer*.

Theofanis G. Stavrou and Peter R. Weisensel: *Russian Travelers to the Christian East from the Twelfth to the Twentieth Century*.

G. Stone and D. S. Worth, eds.: *The Formation of the Slavonic Literary Languages, Proceedings of a Conference Held in Memory of Robert Auty and Anne Pennington at Oxford 6-11 July 1981*.

John W. Strong, ed.: *Essays on Revolutionary Culture and Stalinism (Selected Papers from the Third World Congress for Soviet and East European Studies)*.

Rudolph M. Susel, ed.: *Papers in Slovene Studies 1977*.

Roland Sussex and J. C. Eade, eds.: *Culture and Nationalism in Nineteenth-Century Eastern Europe*.

Oscar E. Swan and Sylvia Gálová-Lorinc: *Beginning Slovak*.

Oscar E. Swan: *First Year Polish*.

Oscar E. Swan: *Intermediate Polish*.

Jane A. Taubman: *A Life Through Poetry   Marina Tsvetaeva's Lyric Diary*.

Charles E. Townsend: *Continuing With Russian*.

Charles E. Townsend: *Czech Through Russian*.

Charles E. Townsend: *A Description of Spoken Prague Czech*.

Charles E. Townsend: *The Memoirs of Princess N. B. Dolgorukaja*.

Charles E. Townsend: *Russian Word Formation*.

Janet G. Tucker: *Innokentij Annenskij and the Acmeist Doctrine*.

Other Books From Slavica

Boryana Velcheva: *Proto-Slavic and Old Bulgarian Sound Changes.*

Walter N. Vickery, ed.: *Aleksandr Blok Centennial Conference.*

Essays in Honor of A. A. Zimin, ed. D. C. Waugh.

Daniel C. Waugh: *The Great Turkes Defiance On the History of the Apocryphal Correspondence of the Ottoman Sultan in its Muscovite and Russian Variants.*

Paul Wexler: *The Ashkenazic Jews: A Slavo-Turkic People in Search of a Jewish Identity.*

Susan Wobst: *Russian Readings and Grammatical Terminology.*

James B. Woodward: *Form and Meaning: Essays on Russian Literature.*

James B. Woodward: *The Symbolic Art of Gogol: Essays on His Short Fiction.*

Dean S. Worth: *Origins of Russian Grammar Notes on the state of Russian philology before the advent of printed grammars.*

Yordan Yovkov: *The Inn at Antimovo* and *Legends of Stara Planina,* translated from Bulgarian by John Burnip.

Что я видел What I Saw by Boris Zhitkov, annotated and edited by Richard L. Leed and Lora Paperno.

Twelve Stories by M. Zoshchenko, selected and annotated for English-speaking students by Lesli LaRocco and Slava Paperno.

JOURNALS

The International Journal of Slavic Linguistics and Poetics.

Folia Slavica

Oral Tradition